Irresistible

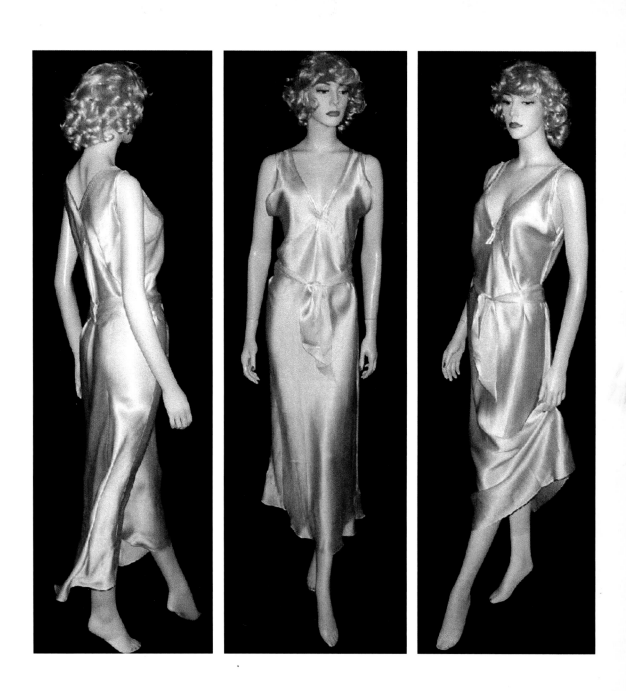

"Underwear makes me
uncomfortable and besides,
my parts have to breathe."

— JEAN HARLOW

Irresistible

The Art of Lingerie

1920s – 1980s

Desire Smith

4880 Lower Valley Road Atglen, Pennsylvania 19310

FRONTISPIECE:
Jean Harlow, "Hollywood's Original Blond Bombshell," one of the most glamorous Hollywood actresses of the 1930s, owned this gown. In pristine condition, with the original hangtag, it is made of silk satin charmeuse. Simply styled and cut on the bias, the full-length gown is not long, as the actress was only slightly over five feet tall.
Courtesy of Richard Reissig.

Helen Turpin

January 12, 1998

To Whom It May Concern:

This note will act as authentication for a peach colored silk 1920's-30's nightgown with attached waist tie, that was owned and worn by Actress Jean Harlow.

I worked for many studios in Hollywood for both movies & television as a make-up and wardrobe consultant. During my employment in the industry, I became friendly with Jean's mother, Mama-Jean Bello after working on a potential project about her daughter.

Mama-Jean was a very kind woman and gave me this nightgown, telling me it had belonged to her daughter.

I attest to the truth in all of the above.

Sincerely,

Helen Turpin 1/12/98
Helen Turpin

5003 Argo Way · Sacramento, California 95820

Author's note: The lingerie included in *Irresistible* is collectors' lingerie, in excellent to never-worn condition. Many pieces were created by well-known designers or have store names adding to the value. Some of the pieces still have the manufacture's hangtags attached to the garment. Regional differences, trends, and economic conditions all affect prices. In determining the price of a particular item of underwear or lingerie, it is appropriate to visit websites that offer lingerie for sale, auctions of antique and vintage clothing (live and Internet), vintage clothing shows, and shops specializing in antique and vintage clothing. Many auctioneers post results online after an auction is held, making it possible to compare images of items sold with prices realized.

Other Schiffer Books By The Author:

Hats, with values
Vintage Style, 1920–1960,
Fashion Footwear, 1800–1970
Fashionable Clothing From The Sears Catalogs, Early 1950s
Fashionable Clothing From The Sears Catalogs, Late 1960s
Fashionable Clothing From The Sears Catalogs, Early 1970s
Handbag Chic, 200 Years of Designer Fashion
Fun Handbags

Designed by Stephanie Daugherty
Type set in Miss Lankfort/Exotc350/Zurich BT
ISBN: 978-0-7643-3930-1
Printed in China

Schiffer Books are available at special discounts for bulk purchases for sales promotions or premiums. Special editions, including personalized covers, corporate imprints, and excerpts can be created in large quantities for special needs. For more information contact the publisher:

Published by Schiffer Publishing Ltd.
4880 Lower Valley Road
Atglen, PA 19310
Phone: (610) 593-1777; Fax: (610) 593-2002
E-mail: Info@schifferbooks.com
For the largest selection of fine reference books on this and related subjects, please visit our website at
www.schifferbooks.com

We are always looking for people to write books on new and related subjects. If you have an idea for a book, please contact us at
proposals@schifferbooks.com

This book may be purchased from the publisher.
Include $5.00 for shipping.
Please try your bookstore first.
You may write for a free catalog.

In Europe, Schiffer books are distributed by
Bushwood Books
6 Marksbury Ave.
Kew Gardens
Surrey TW9 4JF England
Phone: 44 (0) 20 8392 8585; Fax: 44 (0) 20 8392 9876
E-mail: info@bushwoodbooks.co.uk
Website: www.bushwoodbooks.co.uk

In memory of
my dear grandmother,

Eliza Diggle Smith,

who believed that
you cannot have
true glamour
and elegance
without graciousness,
sincerity, and
integrity of character.

Acknowledgments

Special thanks go to Richard Reissig, a retired French horn player and part-time dressmaker for his former colleagues at the New York Metropolitan Opera. Richard added significantly to the book with his fascinating descriptions of the lingerie from his collection. Thanks also go to Laura Brehmer ("Miss Kitty" of The Cats Pajamas Vintage), Shelley Brice-Boyle, Robert Browne (…20th C Apparel), Erin Clune, Nella Daniels, Pamela Daly, Mary Efron, the family of Bernice Harris, Doris Hoagland, Kristen Kucharski, Joel Kuper, a Prominent German Collector, Sascha Joffe, Tyleah Miller, Connie Reissig, Gail and Glenn Sitterly (Time Travelers Antiques and Vintage Clothing), Louise Stewart, and Tess Stewart. I am indebted to Nancy Schiffer for publishing this book and sincere thanks go to Jeffrey Snyder and Bruce Waters at Schiffer Publishing, who did the photography, and Stephanie Daugherty who designed *Irresistible*. Heartfelt thanks as always go to my loved ones and canine companions—*sine qua non*.

Contents

Preface

Lingerie is erotic and provocative. It is about secret delights. It is about the living, breathing, albeit voluptuous, female body. The female body in lingerie is almost bare. Perhaps because of its figure-revealing nature, lingerie is the substance of fantasy, and fantasy is the substance of sex.

Irresistible is about the pleasure of lingerie. It is about the beauty, elegance, and balanced restraint of lingerie, from the early to the latest decades of the twentieth century. The word, "irresistible," is closely tied with the word "urge." Lingerie offers a series of irresistible urges: the urge to buy and possess beautiful lingerie, the urge to wear such lingerie, the deeply sensual urge to touch fine lingerie, and the urge to remove the lingerie, exposing that which was almost bare.

Christian Dior said: "Real elegance is everywhere, especially in things that don't show." Such elegance, such beauty, such pleasure is lingerie. It is irresistible.

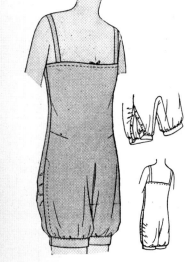

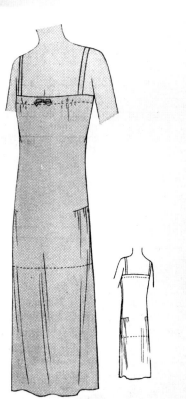

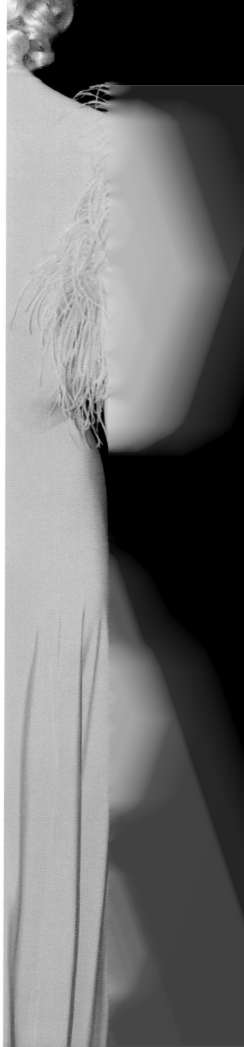

Introduction

James Laver, the noted British costume historian, believes that emphasis in dress tends to shift from one erogenous zone of the body to another. For example, when short hemlines are worn, the legs are in focus; when plunging necklines are worn, the bosom or breasts are emphasized. Although difficult to attach an exact time line to the erogenous zones theory, considering the eclectic nature of contemporary fashion, such a theory definitely relates to lingerie of the 20th-century. Sweeping cultural change relating to the roles of women in society contributed to changes in the design and creation of lingerie during the years between 1920 and 1980.

Men and women of the ancient world wore a loincloth, known in Greece as a perizoma, a length of fabric wrapped around the hips, fitting snugly, not dissimilar to a modern trouser-like undergarment . Some women wore a band to support the breasts

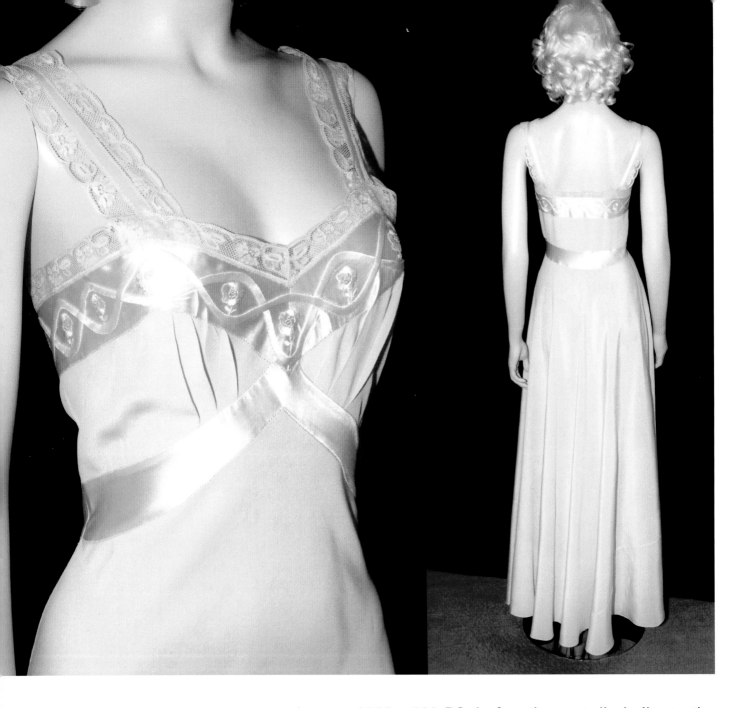

as early as c. 2900 – 300 BC, in function not dissimilar to the modern bra. During the third century AD, the Romans, unlike the Greeks, did not exercise in the gymnasium naked, but wore a modicum of clothing very similar to the modern bikini, or panties and bra. Elizabeth Ewing, in *Dress & Undress*, depicts the first modern bra and briefs in an illustration of a mosaic from the 4th-century AD, from Villa Armerina, Sicily. As a costume historian, I am cognizant of the fact that there is nothing really new in costume. Fashion evolves from previous fashion.

An important change occurred in the early 1920s. As Phyllis G. Tortora and Keith Eubank point out in *Survey of Historic*

Costume: A History of Western Dress, "Never before in the history of costume in the civilized West had women worn skirts that revealed their legs." This very fact changed the design of women's underwear forever.

Not only was the underwear shorter, but during the 1920s colored lingerie came into vogue. The developments made in the dye industry in the early 1920s gradually brought about a general use of what came to be known as the flower tints—tea-rose pink, hydrangea blue, orchid, leaf green, and buttercup yellow. Such colors for lingerie became as popular as the more traditional white, which epitomized the French derivation of the word "lingerie," the word "linge," which means linen. Women's undergarments were originally of linen.

The popularity of the "mannish undergarment," with the same design and construction details as one of the popular styles worn by men and boys of the period, related directly to the general acceptance of tailored and sports clothes for daytime wear. The severity of the style was in direct contrast to the femininity of its wearers.

The word "brassiere" is derived from the French word meaning to bind, to restrain. During the mid-1920s and early 1930s, the object of the brassiere was just that. Whether the brassiere had a straight top or a rounded neckline, its chief purpose was to confine the bust and give an appearance of firmness and trimness to the figure, under the arms and across the back as well.

During the early 1930s, a slip was considered to be the "correct foundation" for a dress, giving a dress "good lines." The slip had to fulfill some very important requirements. It had to be made of material and trimming appropriate for the garment under which it was worn. It had to be scant enough, firm enough, and limp enough not to interfere with the "outer silhouette." It had to be full enough for ease in walking and sitting. Various styles of slips were popular during this period, including the two-piece, the lace-trimmed, the princess, the wrap-around, and the shoulder-dart. Full and half-slips became mini-slips during the 1960s, and then went out of style entirely.

Sleeping garments of the period, included nightgowns, night dresses, and pajamas. Pajamas, a term of Hindu origin, relating to the loose trousers worn by the natives of India, in modern usage refers to a sleeping garment, generally in two pieces, consisting of loose trousers and a roomy coat or over blouse having comparatively straight lines, similar in many respects to the native costume of the Chinese. Although the purpose of sleeping garments is protection and comfort, such aspects as design, trimming, fabric, and color add decorative value and beauty. Some types of nightgowns popular during the mid-1920s include the camisole-top, the empire, the V-neck, the wrap-around, and the "service," strictly tailored and with long sleeves. The pajamas of the period had "foundation" design that could be adjusted and altered to suit many needs. For example, adding long sleeves and a full-length, lapped opening in the front of the top section, makes the pajamas almost a duplicate of a man's outfit, while if a more feminine type was desired, several ruffles of narrow lace were added at the neckline and armholes.

A complete wardrobe of the period, in addition to coats, capes, gowns, dresses, suits, skirts, blouses and lingerie, included a "third type" of garment to be worn in the privacy of one's room. Such garments included the kimono, the negligee, and the bathrobe. As the name signifies, almost all kimonos are cut with kimono sleeves, as is the Japanese national costume from which it is adapted. Fabrication of cotton crepe, figured silk, dotted swiss, taffeta, and challis were widely used in the design and creation of kimonos. The bathrobe usually required a weightier fabrication, such as terry cloth, corduroy, flannel, or soft silk. In purpose similar to the kimono, the negligee is more dainty and elaborate, intended for wear in the intimacy of the home and in the presence of very close friends. Of sheer silk fabrication, frequently trimmed with lace or maribou, most negligees are of a pastel tint. During the late 1960s and into the 1970s sheer garments came out of the bedroom entirely, with the creation of the hostess gown. With a full-length skirt and various styles of bodices, including the halter top, the hostess gown was extremely fashionable. Palazzo pants, fashionable during the 1970s, were not dissimilar to lounging pajamas from the 1920s and early 1930s.

Irresistible provides a comprehensive overview of the types of underwear and lingerie created from 1920 to 1980. Does underwear and lingerie give form to the body or does the body mold its underwear and lingerie? As the silhouette of fashion changes, does underwear and lingerie adapt to the change? From one fashionable decade to another we may not have the same answers to these age-old questions.

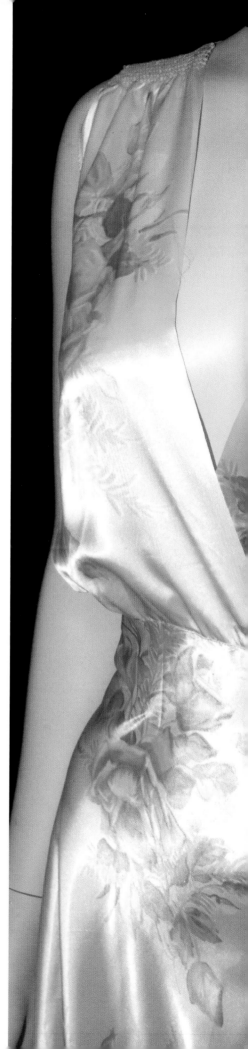

Chapter 1
1920s

A perfect cream silk chiffon teddy with inserted black lace "panels." *Courtesy of Richard Reissig.*

The creator of this black lace and pink silk teddy must have been a poker player! There are two silk diamonds, a silk "spade" and a silk heart in this lingerie "deck." No silk "clubs"! Made during the 1920s, this is a very provocative teddy. *Courtesy of Richard Reissig.*

Absolutely breathtaking is the beautiful silk nightgown and robe ensemble from the early 1920s! Acquired from Nella Daniels, this is Richard Reissig's "signature piece" for *Irresistible*. It is a lingerie work of art! Note the tiny lace pocket on the right hip, the little silk rosebuds, the bi-colored silk ribbons, the belled sleeve ends, and the perfect placement of every piece of lace. *Courtesy of Richard Reissig.*

A rarely seen 1920s one-piece silk lounging pajama. At a glance, this garment appears to be a nightgown, but there are actually two wide legs in the garment. The fabric is a very-fine silk pongee, which is similar to a modern silk crepe-de-chine. The deep armholes and hem are finished with a double-layered net trim. An intricately "carved" rosebud is placed at the bottom of the V neckline. *Courtesy of Richard Reissig.*

RIGHT COLUMN, TOP

A most precious 1920s silk nightgown! One of the most colorful nightgowns of the 1920s, it is a beautiful example of flapper era lingerie "art"! The skirt is golden-peach charmeuse-satin, and the bodice, hip pocket and the shaped hem are green chiffon. *Courtesy of Richard Reissig*.

RIGHT COLUMN, BOTTOM

This gown is cut on the straight-of-grain (not bias cut). Unusually long for its day, it hangs straight from the shoulders. Gowns of this style were often made in one large size or "one size fits all"! *Courtesy of Richard Reissig.*

Made in the style of the "flapper-twenties" is this lovely silk teddy. It is a pull-over style with a buttoned flap pieces between the legs. The teddy was made in recent years for the J. Peterman Company in Lexington, Kentucky. J. Peterman specialized in reproductions of period clothing, and some of their pieces were worn in the Titanic movie. The teddy is made of the finest silk satin, and has never been worn. It even has two tiny rosebuds, so typical of lingerie made in the 1920s. *Courtesy of Richard Reissig.*

BELOW:
Ivory silk teddy with lace of embroidery on net, ivory silk straps and tie at waistline. *Courtesy of …20th C Apparel.*

This is an all-lace slip or chemise that has been converted into a teddy. The buttoned crotch piece is made from a matching color silk, and it could easily be removed. *Courtesy of Richard Reissig.*

A masterpiece of vintage lingerie design is this silk pongee teddy from the Roaring Twenties! It has never been worn, and the silk fabric still retains some of its original crispness. It is a step-in style teddy, meaning that the wearer has to step into the garment before pulling it up to her shoulders. The black lace trim and bi-colored silk ribbon shoulder straps are in perfect condition. *Courtesy of Richard Reissig.*

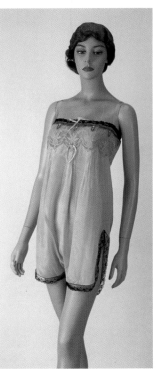

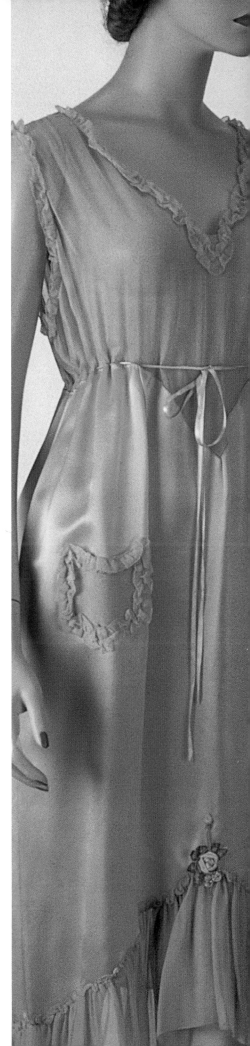

Ankle-length rose silk crepe kimono, with bird and flower design on the skirt, in vibrant and pastel colors; lined with red silk and rose silk crepe. *Courtesy of ...20th C Apparel.*

Ballerina-length lobster pink silk velvet robe, with long, set-in sleeves, in a wrap style, with deep V-neckline and tie at the waistline. *Courtesy of …20ᵗʰ C Apparel.*

Red silk brocade lounging pajamas, with figural images, trees, and flowers, with black silk, with piping on the collar, black silk trimming at hems of trousers, five large black silk knotted buttons, and a black silk sash. *Courtesy of …20ᵗʰ C Apparel. The fitted sleeves suggest that these lounging pajamas were made in China for the European or American markets.*

Two-tone lime green silk crepe lounging pajamas; a three piece set, with blouse, jacket, and trousers. Detailing includes a tie at neckline of blouse and scalloping down the front of the jacket. *Courtesy of …20ᵗʰ C Apparel.*

Chapter 2

1930s

Peach colored silk teddy, with beige lace at the neckline and hem, and beige lace appliqué at the waistline. Labeled *Moon Glow. Author's collection.*

Full-length black silk chiffon nightgown, cut on the bias, with beige lace trim at the hem, neckline, sleeves, and yoke, and beige lace appliqué on the bodice and midriff in a bird and flower motif, with four birds in flight. *Courtesy of …20th C Apparel.*

"The finest clothing made is a person's skin, but, of course, society demands more than this."

— MARK TWAIN

Unusual black cotton lace teddy, with open back, narrow, adjustable straps, some contouring of the brassiere, and a closure of two small mother-of pearl buttons at the crotch. *Author's collection.*

Black silk chiffon and black lace tap panties, with a matching black lace brassiere with narrow black satin straps and a back closure with two hooks and eyes. *Author's collection.*

25

Full-length white cotton batiste nightgown, cut on the bias, with a tulip print in pink, blue, and green, and pink cotton edging at sleeves and V-neckline, with pink bows on the shoulders. *Author's collection*.

A one-piece silk lounging pajama, step-in style, with a small roses print. The neckline and midriff are graced with ecru lace insertions. The blue silk ribbon ties are attached at the front and tied at the back. One or both shoulders have buttons, and this pajama has ties at the back of the neck. *Courtesy of Richard Reissig*.

Full-length peach colored silk damask dressing gown, with a wide collar with beige lace appliqué, fabric-covered buttons, and a sash at the waistline. *Author's collection*.

Pin-tucked green silk chiffon tap panty. It has a six-inch deep hem comprised of an exquisite French lace in a gold color. With a two-button closure at the center back, this panty has never been worn or laundered. *Courtesy of Richard Reissig.*

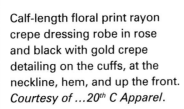

Calf-length floral print rayon crepe dressing robe in rose and black with gold crepe detailing on the cuffs, at the neckline, hem, and up the front. *Courtesy of …20th C Apparel.*

Nathalia-labeled pink silk chiffon robe and gown set from *Bergdorf Goodm*an. The "crown jewel" of Richard Reissig's collection, this beautiful peignoir set is the very essence of feminine boudoir fashion. Both the robe and gown, when laid flat, form full circles! *Courtesy of Richard Reissig.*

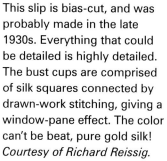

This slip is bias-cut, and was probably made in the late 1930s. Everything that could be detailed is highly detailed. The bust cups are comprised of silk squares connected by drawn-work stitching, giving a window-pane effect. The color can't be beat, pure gold silk! *Courtesy of Richard Reissig.*

Intimate apparel can sometimes be very funny! Here is a 1930s silk chiffon tap panty with the word "frou" appearing on each leg! Frivolous indeed! *Courtesy of Richard Reissig, from the collection of Pamela Daly.*

Coral-red silk crepe bra and tap panty set, with golden lace for the bra cups and hem of panty. A fun piece of lingerie! Note the scalloping where silk and lace combine, and again at the lace hem. *Courtesy of Richard Reissig.*

"Most Glorious" very lacy and silk satin nightgown. Never has there been seen a vintage silk nightgown with so much lace over the upper and lower parts of the gown! The gown is essentially "backless," leaving only the middle of the torso covered by pure silk satin. *Courtesy of Richard Reissig.*

This period of costume history is truly characterized by feminine boudoir elegance!

This is clearly a haute couture silk robe. The robe remains the best of its kind in Richard Reissig's extensive robe collection. There is an abundance of French lace throughout the robe, and the garment was made with extreme care. The gown was made in the early 1930s, as evidenced by the presence of an "NRA" label (National Reclamation Act under President Roosevelt). The robe has never been worn. *Courtesy of Richard Reissig*.

A wonderful silk crepe-de-chine nightgown made by *Madelon* in Paris. The bodice is made of corded French lace, and the skirt is cut on the bias for a great clingy look. *Courtesy of Richard Reissig.*

This gown is "local" to Pennsylvania, having been sold by the famous John Wanamaker store in Philadelphia. A distinctive wide-skirted *Fischer* silk nightgown, made from semi-sheer silk georgette, its side seams have been replaced by two-inch wide lace panels. There is not much known about the Fischer Lingerie Company itself. Fischer originated in the late 1930s and their office was located in New York City. They became famous for the use of lace in the bodice of both nightgowns and slips. Many of the slips used lace shoulder straps and many of the nightgowns had back necklines that were cut below the waistline. *Courtesy of Richard Reissig.*

Perfectly matched silk satin nightgown and two-piece pajama set. The two pieces have identical lace ruffles at the bodices and at the hems. They were very likely made as designer samples and never sold at retail. *Courtesy of Richard Reissig.*

This black silk chiffon nightgown has red flowers appliquéed on the bodice and red piping along the neckline. The chiffon fabric is very sheer and very revealing. Made in the 1930s, provocative gowns like this one are very rare and highly prized by vintage lingerie collectors. *Courtesy of Richard Reissig.*

Most of the bodice and the left side of the skirt is lace, and the rest of the gown is "cobwebby" silk chiffon. Worn with a long slip, the gown would be just fine as an evening dress. *Courtesy of Richard Reissig*.

Franklin Simon "Underthings Shop"
silk nightgown with appliqués and lace.
Courtesy of Richard Reissig.

39

A very sheer rayon chiffon and lace nightgown, it has a totally-sheer lace bodice and a 13-inch deep lace hem. *Courtesy of Richard Reissig.*

Black sheer silk georgette gown.
Courtesy of a Prominent German Collector.

41

Pink silk *Fischer* gown with a half-circle skirt, full chiffon sleeves and a very dramatic lace and chiffon bodice. *Courtesy of a Prominent German Collector.*

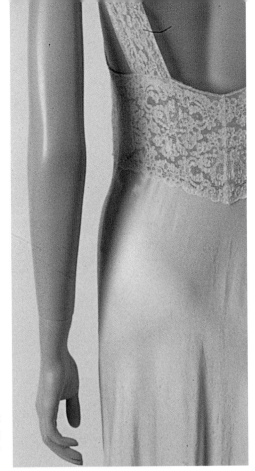

Pink silk gown, with outside sewn bust darts which is most unusual. *Courtesy of Sascha Joffe.*

"Lady Love" very sheer black silk chiffon gown. *Courtesy of Richard Reissig.*

Pink silk charmeuse gown with shoulder holes. *Courtesy of Pamela Daly and Richard Reissig.*

"Simper ubi sub ubi."
(always wear underwear)

—ANDREW RIDINGS

"Hanky Panky Panty" with handkerchief hem. A fun piece of lingerie! *Courtesy of Pamela Daly and Richard Reissig.*

Full-length *Lady Duff* (Gordon) dressing gown; cream silk chiffon and cream silk satin, also insertion at waistline of needle lace on fine net and silk ribbon. Labeled *Lady Duff, Paris, New York. Author's collection.*

Lady Duff was a real person. Along with her husband, Lord Duff, they were rescued passengers on the ill-fated steamship Titanic.

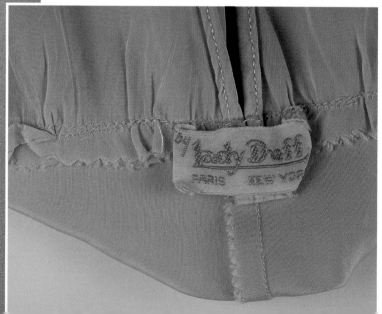

Golden lace teddy with pink silk chiffon bodice and skirt, godet insertions. Made to show! *Courtesy of Richard Reissig.*

Semi-sheer rayon georgette nightgown in a brilliant cabbage roses print. Made by *Radcliffe,* this bias cut gown has never been worn. *Courtesy of Richard Reissig*.

Ivory silk nightgown with lace appliqué on a double-layer net bodice. An exceptional piece, this gown must have been custom-made for a tall woman. It is sixty-eight inches in total length! *Courtesy of Richard Reissig.*

Although cut in the same way as other wide-skirted gowns shown in *Irresistible*, this beautiful nightgown is made of exceptionally fine-quality rayon crepe-de-chine fabric. The color is carnation pink, and note the very large scallops in the hem of the gown. *Courtesy of Richard Reissig.*

This is a delightful and airy rayon georgette floral print nightgown. The gown shares the same cut as the other gowns with half-circle skirts in this book. *Courtesy of Richard Reissig.*

Floral printed bias-cut rayon nightgown. *Courtesy of Richard Reissig.*

This *Lady Duff* labeled nightgown has a sweeping, half-circle skirt. The fabric is a semi-sheer rayon georgette fabric, accented with a satin neckline and large satin midriff piece. *Courtesy of Richard Reissig.*

Custom hand-dyed (after manufacture) in a variety of earth-tone colors, is this rayon crepe-de-chine nightgown. Hand-dying a rayon (or silk) gown in this manner does not harm the fabric. The soft luster and pleasant "feel" of the fabric is retained. The skirt of this gown is very full, and the armholes are cut right to the waistline. *Courtesy of Richard Reissig.*

Cut in the same manner as the "earth-tones" dyed gown, this nightgown was made from a hot-pink silk chiffon fabric. The *Barbara Lee* label appears in the gown. *Courtesy of a Prominent German collector.*

Chapter 3
1940s

Matching nightgown and slip made by *FrayPruf* from *Bur-Mil (Burlington Mills)* rayon fabric. Both slip and gown have matching Art Deco style necklines, and also share the same "coat of arms" appliqué on the left side of the bodice. Neither piece has ever been worn and the slip has the original paper hangtag. *Courtesy of Richard Reissig.*

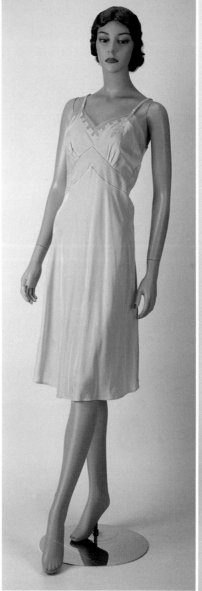

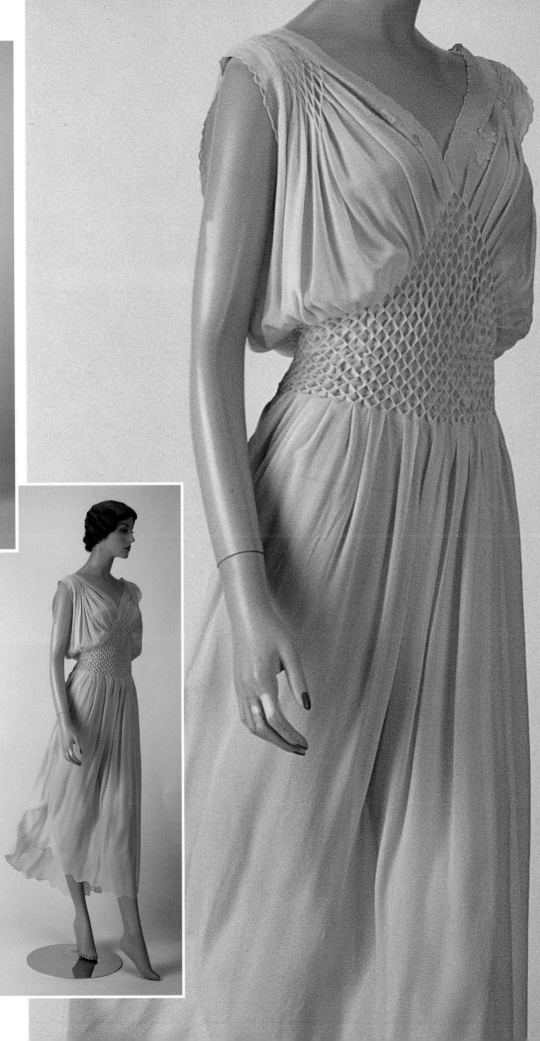

This never-worn silk chiffon nightgown has unique "waffle" pattern smocking all around the midriff and at the shoulders. The garment is the same width (45 inches) from shoulder to hem; the only shaping provided by the smocking. No elastic is used. The smocking threads are intertwined in such a manner as to provide for a range of waist sizes. Other details include a "quintuple"-scalloped hem, five small scallops are part of a larger scallop. Gowns of this design originated in pre-war Japan, but this one was "Hand Made" in Hong Kong. *Courtesy of Richard Reissig.*

If ever there was a "perfect negligee," this 100% silk taffeta robe could be exactly that! It was made by *Perfect Negligee* in New York, and is in perfect, never-worn condition. The skirt has a most amazing sweep of over 300 inches along the hem. The garment has a silk organdy crinoline, which adds greatly to the fullness of the skirt. The dolman-type sleeves are gathered at the elbows, and a corded silk belt pulls in the fullness around the waist. It truly is a glamorous robe in the best tradition of Hollywood glamour! *Courtesy of Richard Reissig*.

A very fancy slip from the 1940s! This slip has the most lace and satin detailing that we've ever seen. Clearly, the slip was meant to be seen and not covered up. It is new/old stock, and still bears its original price tag of only $4.98! Manufactured by *Miss Deb. Courtesy of Richard Reissig.*

A pretty blue rayon slip called the *Madi Slip*. It was made by *Madison Lingerie* during the World War II years, and still bears it's paper care tag. Slips made during this period usually had fancy lace detailing at the bodice and hem. They were often worn under sheer blouses. This slip is new/old stock. *Courtesy of Richard Reissig.*

Pink silk crepe-de-chine "Strawberries" gown, designed by *Hattie Carnegie*. A rare gown, with silk satin trim and delicately embroidered strawberries on the bodice, and the designer's label stitched inside. *Courtesy of Richard Reissig and Joel Kuper.*

A most colorful floral print nightgown and robe ensemble made of a heavier weight rayon satin! Made by *Radcliffe*, the cabbage roses print is exactly the same as that in the *Radcliff* georgette gown shown elsewhere in Irresistible. *Courtesy of Richard Reissig.*

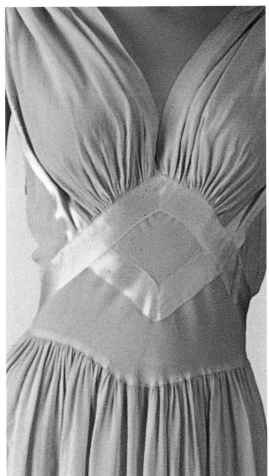

A Grecian-inspired silk chiffon nightgown made by *Fischer*. Although not bias-cut, the skirt is gathered into a diamond-patterned midriff panel. *Courtesy of Richard Reissig.*

"Scottie dogs" never worn pink silk charmeuse gown. On the left breast there is an embroidered figure of two kissing "Scottie dogs"! At the bottom of the front neckline is a dog bone patch. *Courtesy of Richard Reissig.*

Juel Park custom made tailored chocolate-brown silk slip. *Courtesy of Richard Reissig.*

Juel Park custom-made couture silk satin robe, with silk crepe-de-chine full lining, and a kitten patch-appliqué over the right breast. *Courtesy of Richard Reissig.*

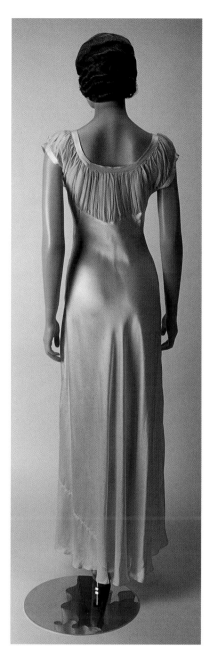

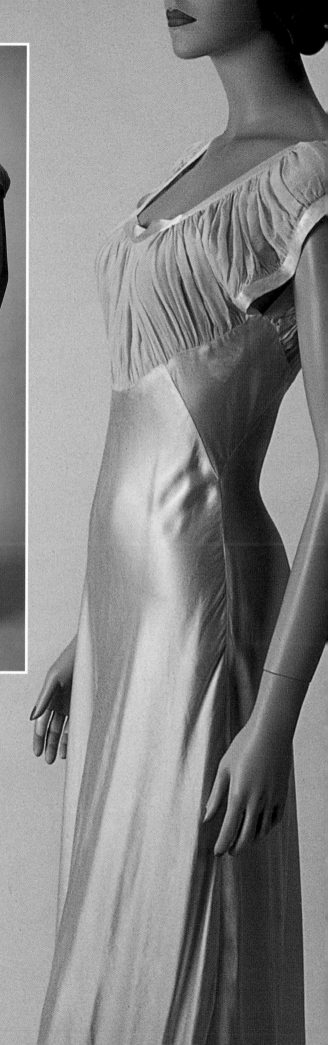

Silk charmeuse *Fischer* nightgown, with a silk chiffon bodice.
Courtesy of Richard Reissig, acquired from Gail and Glenn Sitterly,
Time Travelers.

Hatem labeled black silk satin gown. A treasure, this is a fine example of the haute couture nightgowns of the period! *Courtesy of Richard Reissig.*

A stunning silk satin boudoir ensemble that has never been worn! Several design elements stand out; the cowl neckline and the shoulder ties of the gown. The robe has five tucks made in the upper part of the sleeves, thus creating an unusual slanted opening for the arms. It's a wrap-style robe, with the waist ties coming around to meet at the center back. The set was likely custom-made, as there is only a tag stating: "100% Pure Silk – Size 15". *Courtesy of Richard Reissig.*

Off-white silk chiffon nightgown with a half-circle skirt and a small dot pattern in the fabric. *Courtesy of Richard Reissig.*

An "unforgettable" black rayon crepe-de-chine nightgown! It has "Forget-Me-Not" flowers (words also) embroidered across the front of the gown. Corded white piping along the shoulder straps, and along the front and back necklines. *Courtesy of Richard Reissig.*

Another showpiece of *Fischer* extravagance! The gown features four-inch wide lace panels in an inverted V or chevron pattern. This same lace appears on the back of the bodice, dipping well-below the waistline. *Fischer* also made this same gown in black silk chiffon. *Courtesy of Richard Reissig.*

This closely-fitted crepe-back satin dressing gown was made by *Flobert*. This is a heavier grade of satin with a very shiny surface finish. Most true dressing gowns were step-in style with zipper closure beginning at the knee level. Not restricted to the boudoir, this gown serves well as a hostess gown. *Courtesy of a Prominent German Collector.*

A beautifully shaped bodice with much gathering, front and back, features this never-worn *Fischer* silk nightgown. *Courtesy of Richard Reissig.*

This fine rayon satin nightgown with a muted floral print has a free-swinging half-circle skirt. *Courtesy of a Prominent German Collector.*

A superb pink silk chiffon nightgown with a half-circle skirt and squared neckline. The bodice is figuratively encrusted with delicate ecru lace, and three large silk-satin flowers are inserted over each breast. *Courtesy of Richard Reissig.*

A fine silk georgette gown, with a deeply-cut lacy back. The front bodice is also low-cut, and the gown has a very-full, half-circle skirt. *Courtesy of Richard Reissig*.

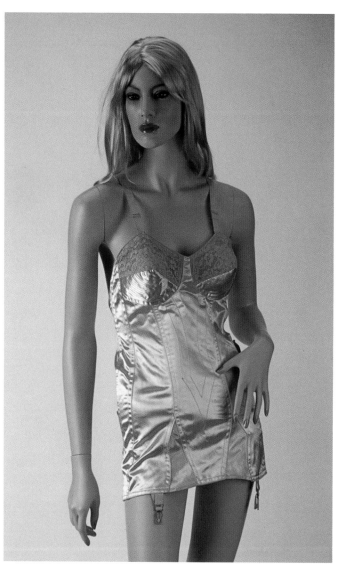

Pale peach satin combination, with circle-stitched lace and satin brassiere cups, decorative stitching on front panel and seams, and a zipper closure partially up one side. Additionally detailed with hooks and eyes, grosgrain ribbon straps, with an open bottom style, with elastic, rubber, and metal garters. *Courtesy of …20th C Apparel.*

Full-length burgundy satin dressing gown, with trapunto quilting in a floral design on the bodice, and on the short, cuffed sleeves, five fabric-covered buttons on the bodice and a wrap skirt, tying at the waistline. Labeled *B. Altman & Co., Paris, New York*. *Courtesy of …20th C Apparel.*

Peach colored satin step-in dressing gown, with trapunto quilting in a floral design on the short sleeves of the fitted bodice, ties at the neckline and waistline, and zipper partially up the front of the flared skirt. *Author's collection*.

Lounging pajamas, with rose satin blouse with quilting on the collar and gold-tone buttons, and black trousers, labeled *Miss Fashion*. *Courtesy of ...20th C Apparel.*

Full-length aqua, gray, and white wool plaid robe, in a double breasted style, with patch pockets, with a gray satin monogram, "LH," on the breast pocket. *Author's collection.*

Tess Stewart models red star print rayon nightgown. Labeled *Pandora*. *Courtesy of ...20th C Apparel.*

Pink satin brassiere with circle stitching. Labeled *Quest Shon Mark, 38C*. Courtesy of …*20th C Apparel*. Similar styles were fashionable into the early 1950s, making this difficult to accurately date.

Full-length ivory satin dressing gown, with a floral pattern of red roses with green leaves. *Author's collection*.

Tyleah Miller models a classic peach colored silk slip from the 1940s, with beige lace appliqué and insertion. The straps are adjustable. *Author's collection*.

73

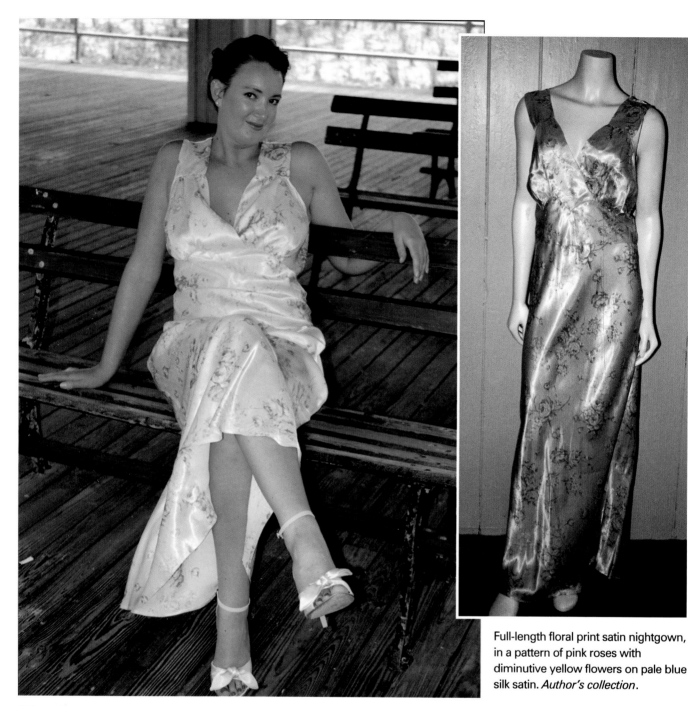

Kristen Kucharski models a floral print satin nightgown.

Full-length floral print satin nightgown, in a pattern of pink roses with diminutive yellow flowers on pale blue silk satin. *Author's collection*.

"A lady is one who never shows her underwear unintentionally."

—LILLIAN DAY

Ivory satin dressing gown, with ivory lace appliqué on the shoulders and short sleeves, and a wrap style skirt, tying at the waistline. *Author's collection.*

"Girl In The Seamprufe Slip" white rayon crepe-de-chine slip. A simple, pretty, never-worn slip, with a rare manufacturer's hangtag! *Courtesy of Richard Reissig.*

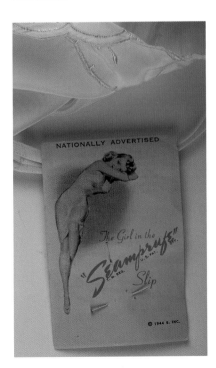

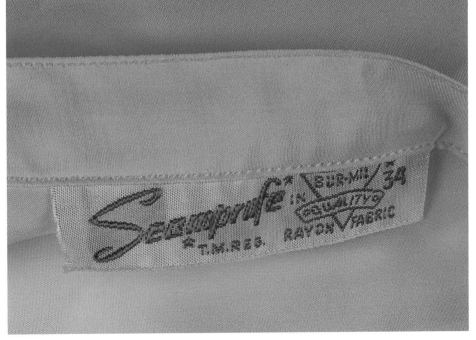

Van Raalte "Stryps" peach rayon teddy or "onesie," with alternating stripes exactly the same, "Stryp-to-Stryp," but every other stripe is knit at a different angle to its neighbor. The *Van Raalte* series of knit rayon "Stryps" are unique in their design and collectability. *Courtesy of Richard Reissig.*

Van Raalte "Stryps" silver pink knit rayon nightgown. *Courtesy of Richard Reissig.*

Van Raalte "Stryps" peach knit rayon nightgown. *Courtesy of Richard Reissig*.

Van Raalte "Stryps" aqua blue knit rayon nightgown. *Courtesy of Richard Reissig*.

Van Raalte "Stryps" golden-yellow knit rayon nightgown. *Courtesy of Richard Reissig*.

Full-length black silk chiffon nightgown with black lace bodice, gathered into two circles at the bust, with an open triangle at the waistline, and wide, black lace straps. Labeled *Oppenheim Collins*. *Author's collection*.

Chapter 4
1950s

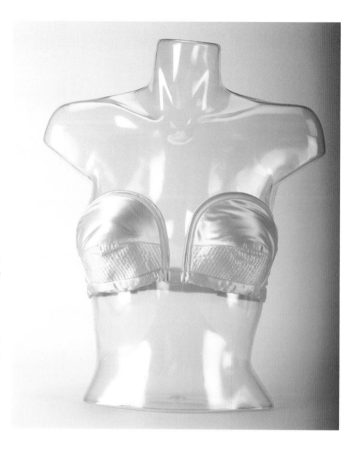

Ivory rayon satin strapless brassiere, under-wire style with light padding, and waffle pattern stitching on bottom half of cups, elastic and double hook and eye closure in back. Labeled *Secret Charm by Marvelform, Rayon, 34A, 1950s*. The original box states that *Sears Charmode Brassieres, Secret Charm by Marvelform, Charmode Brassieres Are Sold Only By Sears, Roebuck And Company*, PAT NOS 2538864, 2333434. *Courtesy of ...20th C Apparel*.

"Are you there God? It's me, Margaret. I just told my mother I want a bra. Please help me grow God. You know where. I want to be like everyone else."

— JUDY BLUME

Couture silk chiffon nightgown made by *Aïda Spilo* in New York. The skirt is very, very wide, forming a half circle when laid out flat. Tiny self-fabric cords comprise the shoulder pieces and the waist ties. A truly magnificent piece of vintage lingerie! *Courtesy of Richard Reissig.*

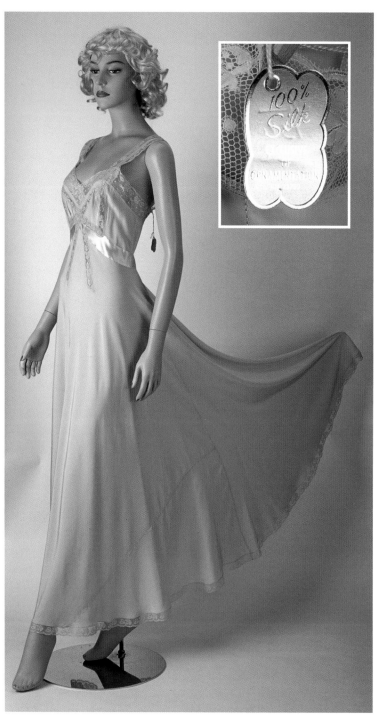

This pink silk crepe-de-chine nightgown bears both *Neiman-Marcus* store label, and a gilt *"100% Silk"* hangtag. *Courtesy of Richard Reissig.*

A very-glamorous silk charmeuse nightgown, paired with a very plush rayon velvet coat. This ensemble was made by *Jonquil* and sold by *Neiman-Marcus*. The gown and robe share the most exquisite Point de Venise lace. The robe displays this lace on the shoulders and on the cuffs. The front bodice of the nightgown is literally encrusted with this spectacular lace, while the back bodice is sheer silk chiffon. The skirt of the gown is a full half-circle, and there is only one seam at the center-back. *Courtesy of Richard Reissig. Exceptionally beautiful ensemble!*

Black nylon and cotton strapless bustier or torsolette, decorated with black eyelet lace appliqué and red satin embroidered laces, with elastic insertion, boning, hooks and eyes. Labeled *Hollywood Vassarette, V-ette. Author's collection.*

"I felt oddly as if I were doing something illegal, something that might land me in hell, something my prune-faced 4th grade teacher Sister Estelle would surely frown upon. I guarantee you, she would give me a hard whack with her ruler if she knew what naughty number I tried on."

—Monica Murphy Lemoine
(Knocked Up, Knocked Down)

Red and white speckled print cotton and rayon camisole, with boning, wide, fabric straps, and a zipper up the front. Labeled *Gossard*. *Author's collection*.

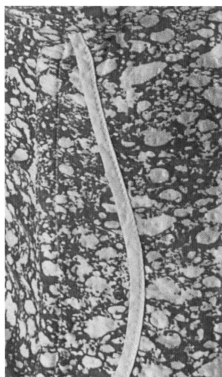

Pink silk crepe-de-chine *Neiman Marcus* half-slip which matches the *Neiman-Marcus* pink silk nightgown shown elsewhere in this book. The never-worn slip has a 6-1/2 inch lace hem with satin "diamond" insertions, French seams, and an elasticized back waistline. *Courtesy of Richard Reissig.*

Red elastic and red satin open-bottom girdle, with black satin with metal garters, decorative black stitching, and red lace bow appliqué. Labeled *Curtis, Eddyform, Rayon, Cotton, Rubber, Large 1870. Courtesy of ...20th C Apparel*.

Red ruffled stiff nylon crinoline. Labeled *Styled by Florell*. *Author's collection*.

White cotton, elastic, and rubber long-line bra, described as a "6 Way Brassiere," with front "hooks and eyes" closure. Labeled *Splendor Form Brassiere Co., N. Y. Author's collection.*

Pale pink stiff net crinoline, with a pink satin ruffle at the hem. *Author's collection.*

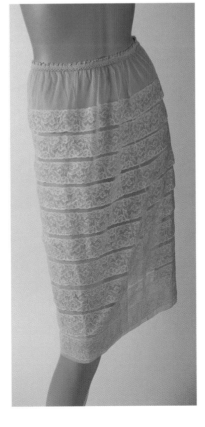

Ballerina Tess Stewart on toes wearing pink net crinoline.

White nylon half-slip, with horizontal ruffles of lace, from just below the waistline to the slightly flared hem. *Author's collection.*

Two pale pink quilted satin bed jackets, by *Barbizon*. *Author's collection.*

Although very few contemporary women wear bed jackets, they were very fashionable during the 1940s and 1950s, when many women rested in bed while reading. These jackets are beautifully tailored, and are excellent with a gown for evening wear, or for day wear, with pants.

Ivory net crinoline, with horizontal bands of ivory satin, a white nylon yoke, and elasticized waistband. *Author's collection.*

Sheer white net crinoline, with a ruffle at the hem. *Author's collection.*

Pink polished cotton jacket, with quilted peplum and collar, and rhinestones detailing the belt. *Courtesy of …20th C Apparel. The design of this robe references skating attire of the period.*

Kristen Kucharski models black and white satin brassiere and garter belt.

Black and white satin push-up style brassiere, with lace and ribbon insertion, and matching garter belt. *Courtesy of 20ᵗʰ C Apparel.*

"The idea is treating lingerie like a real garment – it's very chic to see your underwear now, especially a bra. I wear great bras I know people will see under sheer blouses."

— LAUREN GOODMAN

Black and pink nylon tulle, net, and lace nightgown, with black velvet tie-straps. *Courtesy of …20th C Apparel.*

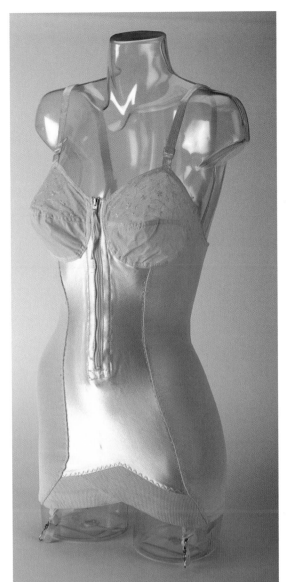

White satin, nylon spandex, and lace open bottom combination with garters, and a zipper partially up the front. Labeled *Q-T Foundation, 36B. Courtesy of …20th C Apparel.*

Left, ballerina-length pale pink sheer nylon nightgown, with a fitted bodice with pink lace appliqué, and a full skirt , gathered at the waistline. Labeled *Shadowline;*

Right, ballerina-length white sheer nylon nightgown, with a fitted bodice with beige and pale green floral lace appliqué, and a full skirt, gathered and tied at the waistline. Labeled *Van Raalte, All Nylon. Author's collection.*

Black satin, lace, and elastic bustier or torsolette, with wire frame and back closure with metal hooks and eyes. Labeled *Perma lift, A Stein & Company, Chicago, New York, Los Angeles. Author's collection.*

Black strapless brassiere with circle stitching on black satin and black net, and a wire "frame." *Courtesy of …20th C Apparel.*

Black spandex, cotton, acetate, and nylon girdle, with garters, with black tulle trim at the hem, and a satin panel in back, with decorative black scrolling. Labeled *Oblique By Tru Balance, Made In U.S.A. Author's collection.*

"The birthday suit is best, lingerie just makes it more exciting!"

— MOOPAK (CURRENT.COM)

Gold quilted satin calf-length robe, with jeweled buttons, and tan, gold, and white paisley brocade trim. Labeled *Style 5839*. *Author's collection*.

This is a silk crepe-de-chine two-piece pajama which bears the *Neiman-Marcus* store label. Note the satin medallions which comprise the yoke, sleeve cuffs and the hip pocket. *Courtesy of Richard Reissig*.

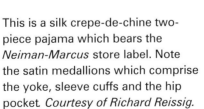

Pink silk full slip is part of this very unique group of never-worn *Neiman-Marcus* pieces. This slip also has the *Neiman-Marcus* gilt hangtag. Note the tiny box pleats in the bodice. The cups are silk satin, as is the entire back of the bodice. *Courtesy of Richard Reissig*.

Chapter 5
1960s

Kristen Kucharski models a stylized floral print nylon hostess dress, with a fashionable mock-halter neckline. *Author's collection*.

BOTTOM ROW:
Left: Nylon floral print set, with calf-length dressing gown, with short sleeves and yoke trimmed with black lace; Right: Ankle-length nightgown, with black lace insertion on the bodice, and lace trim on the sleeves and at the hem. Labeled *Vanity Fair, Made In U.S.A. Author's collection*.

Ankle-length nylon print nightgown, with blue polka dots on white, and diagonal stripes in fuchsia, tan and blue, a camisole bodice with an elevated waistline and spaghetti straps. Labeled *Vassarette, Made In U.S.A. Author's collection*.

Ankle-length nylon floral print nightgown, with large mint green and coral color poppies on navy blue, an elevated waistline with drawstring, and spaghetti straps. Labeled *Lorraine, 100% Nylon. Author's collection.*

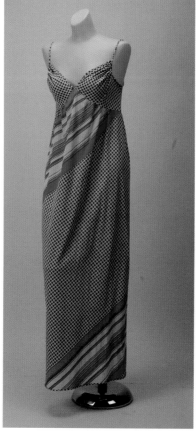

Bra slip or bandeau slip, with a black nylon lace, elastic, and acetate top with a black nylon skirt, trimmed at the hem with black lace. Labeled *Kayser, Made In U.S.A. Author's collection*.

Ankle-length two-tone purple nylon nightgown, with a deep V-neckline, detailed with two small buttons and a bow, an open back that ties at the neckline, and an elasticized waistline. *Author's collection*.

White nylon ankle-length nightgown in a softly pleated Grecian style, with beige lace trim at the neckline, around the armholes, and at the midriff. Labeled *Yolande, Nylon Tricot, 34. Courtesy ...20th C Apparel*.

"Lingerie, remember lingerie?"

—BRUCE SPENCE
(*MAD MAX 2: THE ROAD WARRIOR*)

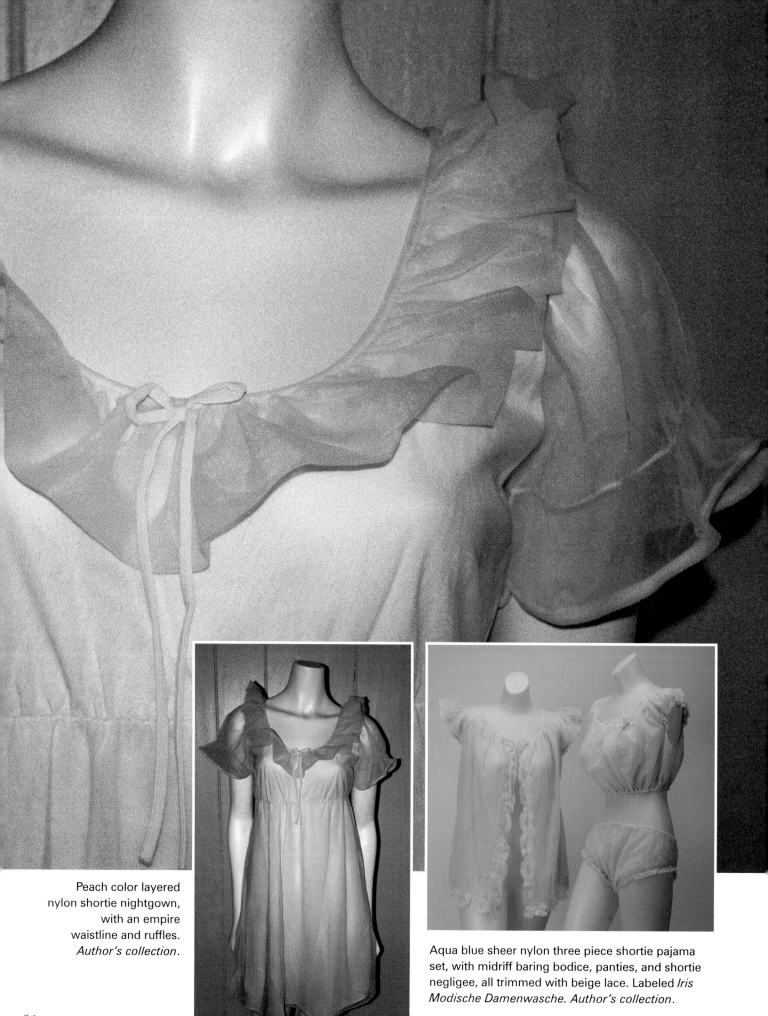

Peach color layered nylon shortie nightgown, with an empire waistline and ruffles. *Author's collection*.

Aqua blue sheer nylon three piece shortie pajama set, with midriff baring bodice, panties, and shortie negligee, all trimmed with beige lace. Labeled *Iris Modische Damenwasche. Author's collection*.

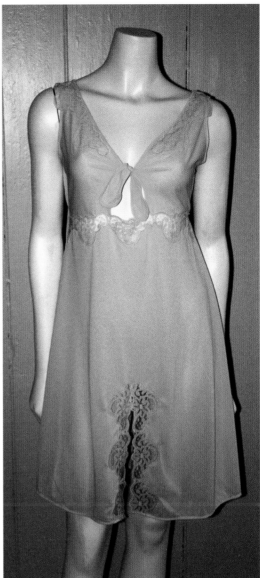

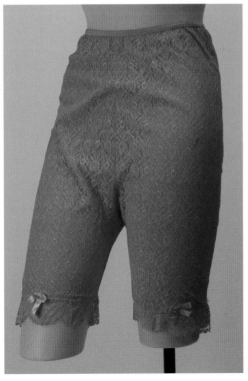

Left, chartreuse nylon slip, with beige lace appliqué on the bodice and trim at the hem. Labeled *Van Raalte*;

Right, colorful floral print sheer nylon mini slip or mini-petti, in tan, fuchsia, orange, and green. Label removed, most likely by *Vanity Fair*. *Author's collection*.

Although full slips are not being worn as often as they were in the 1960s, these colorful nylon vintage slips make wonderful summer nightgowns.

Pink nylon shortie nightgown, with a tie and lace appliqué and insertion on the bodice, and lace insertion at the hem. Labeled *100% Nylon. Author's collection.*

Coral pink nylon lace pettipants, with ruffles and satin bows at the cuffs. *Author's collection*.

Kristen Kucharski models the sheer nylon mini slip from the 1960s.

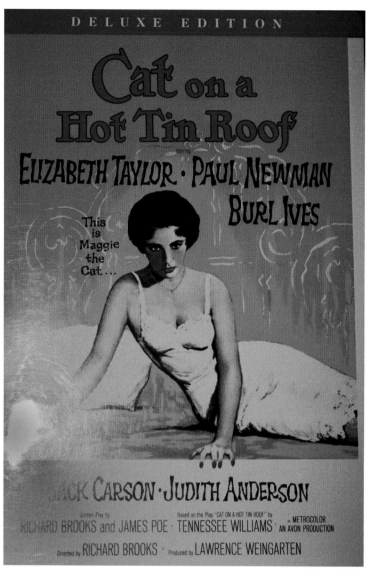

"I often think that a slightly exposed shoulder emerging from a long satin nightgown packed more sex than two naked bodies in bed."

— BETTE DAVIS

Soft pink ankle-length wool crepe gown, trimmed at the yoke, hem, and elbow-length sleeves with dyed pink marabou feathers, with a sash, and white silk chiffon lining. Labeled *Karam, New York, Nan Duskin*. *Courtesy of the Family of Bernice Harris.*

Pale blue two-layered nylon ankle-length nightgown, with beige lace trim on the bodice and at the hem, pale blue satin spaghetti straps, iridescent pink rhinestone detailing, and a narrow blue satin sash inserted at the waistline. Labeled *Lucie Ann, Beverly Hills*. *Courtesy of the Family of Bernice Harris.*

Pale blue and red nylon shortie nightgown, with bandana-inspired bodice and blue denim twill-inspired skirt, white nylon edging, and matching panties. Labeled *Katz Mini Gown, 100% Nylon*. *Author's collection*.

Nylon floral printed shortie nightgown, trimmed at the neckline with white satin, and at the hem with white lace, with an all over tulip pattern in yellow, pink, lilac and white, with additional white satin tulip appliqué. Labeled *Lucie Ann, Made In U.S.A*. *Author's collection*.

Left, bright yellow nylon shortie nightgown, edged with white nylon, labeled *Vassearette, 100% Antron Nylon Tricot*; Right, ankle-length pale yellow nylon and satin nightgown, with an elevated waistline, a white lace bodice with a yellow nylon bow and yellow nylon spaghetti straps, and a full skirt. *Author's collection*.

Although shortie nightgowns were popular during the late 1950s, the shortie nightgowns with gathering, openwork, and tight fitting or bikini panties, as opposed to bloomer-style panties, did not become fashionable until the 1960s.

This flirty short silk nightgown was made for *Neiman-Marcus*. It is a complete style departure from the other *Neiman-Marcus* pieces. The focus here is on the brilliant red-orange color of the silk. *Courtesy of Richard Reissig.*

Left, knee-length bright green sheer nylon nightgown, with ruffles at the scoop neckline and at the hem; Right, knee-length blue nylon "feather print" nightgown, with cape sleeves tying at the shoulders. Labeled *Travel-Lite For Saks Fifth Avenue*. *Author's collection*.

Sheer lavender nylon shortie nightgown, trimmed at the neckline, hem, and panties with white marabou feathers. *Author's collection*.

Hot pink two-layered nylon ankle-length nightgown, with a Grecian style bodice, trimmed with gold brocade, and a full skirt with a deep ruffle at the hem, and gold brocade detailing on the skirt of the inner layer. Labeled *Eye-ful*. Courtesy of the Family of Bernice Harris.

Demure pink nylon ballerina-length nightgown, with a camisole bodice, appliquéd with beige nylon lace, diminutive rhinestones and pearls, spaghetti straps in clusters of three, a harem skirt and second layer of nylon. Labeled *Vanity Fair*. *Courtesy of the Family of Bernice Harris.*

Full-length demure pale blue nylon satin robe and matching nightgown, elaborately trimmed with ruffles and white nylon lace, and with a sash at the waistline. Labeled *Givenchy – Intimite, Paris*. *Courtesy of the Family of Bernice Harris.*

Warm pink satin crepe full-length robe, trimmed at the sleeves and neckline with beige lace. Labeled *Lanvin, Paris, New York*. *Courtesy of the Family of Bernice Harris.*

Full-length pink velour robe scattered with pink rhinestones, with a flared hem, elbow-length sleeves, a scoop neckline, zipper partially up the back, and a belt with snap closure. Labeled *Perfect Negligee, New York*. *Courtesy of the Family of Bernice Harris.*

Salmon pink nylon crepe full-length robe and matching nightgown, both with elaborate ruffles, gown with Juliet lines and spaghetti straps. Labeled *Lebis*. *Courtesy of the Family of Bernice Harris.*

Black lace brassiere, under wire style, with a small, pink rayon bow, adjustable black satin straps, and black elastic back closure with a single hook and eye, labeled *Secret Fulfillment by Lilyette, 32B, Non-Elastic Sections 100% Nylon*. Courtesy of ...20th C Apparel.

"She found this vintage 1950s bra and slip with the tags still on it and told me back then that it was my 'Maggie the cat' costume. We're using the bra in the play now."

—ANGIE HARRELL

Coffee color nylon slip, with beige lace appliqué. *Author's collection. Nylon, introduced at the New York World's Fair in 1939, was diverted for military use during World Wart II. Although in general use for lingerie during the 1950s, solid color nylon slips, panties, and half-slips did not become fashionable until the early 1960s.*

Leopard print brassiere in stretch fabric of 71% nylon and 29% Lycra Spandex, labeled *Vanity Fair, Made In U. S. A. 34B. Courtesy of ...20ᵗʰ C Apparel.*

Leopard print panty girdle of nylon and Lycra Spandex, labeled *Vanity Fair, Made In U. S. A. Courtesy of ...20ᵗʰ C Apparel.*

Leopard print spandex and nylon girdle with garters. Labeled *Vanity Fair. Courtesy of the Family of Bernice Harris.*

Kristen Kucharski models beige nylon tap panties and bustier.

Black elastic and nylon lace bustier or torsolette, with a wire frame, partial circle stitching, black tulle ruffle, and back closure with metal hooks and eyes. Labeled *Caprice of Hollywood*. Author's collection.

Left, black nylon lace and elastic bustier or torsolette, with loops for garters. Labeled *I owe it all to Goddess*; Right, black nylon lace knee-length nightgown, with a deep scoop neckline and black lace straps with pink ribbon insertion. Labeled *Movie Star, Made In U.S.A. Author's collection*.

"If love is blind, why is lingerie so popular?"

—SOURCE UNKNOWN

Coffee color and brown polka dot printed nylon bikini panties. Labeled *Radiant, Bonwit Teller*, purchased in 1966. *These panties were in a cardboard tube, with two additional pairs. Author's collection*

Spandex and nylon hi-rise panty girdle, in a bold, colorful floral print. Labeled *Vanity Fair*. *Courtesy of the Family of Bernice Harris.*

Sheer beige nylon tap panty, with fine black lace appliqué, and scalloped hems with black lace. Labeled *Vanity Fair* (sheer label with gold embroidery). *Author's collection.*

Floral print spandex and nylon girdle with garters. Labeled *Vanity Fair*. *Courtesy of the Family of Bernice Harris.*

"Brevity is the soul of lingerie."

— DOROTHY PARKER

Left, sheer red nylon slip, with red lace and pleating on the bodice and at the hem. Labeled *100% Nylon, California Lingerie Co.*; Right, red nylon pettipants, trimmed with black lace. Labeled *Charmode. Author's collection.*

"What's the worst
that can happen?
If it doesn't do well
I can put on my big girl panties,
deal with it and move on."

— HALLE BERRY

Red lace, elastic, and rayon
garter belt/panties, labeled
Princess Foundations.
*Courtesy of
...20ᵗʰ C Apparel.*

Reversible ballerina-length red and ivory silk brocade dressing gown, in a wrap style with bell sleeves. *Most likely made in Hong Kong. Author's collection.*

"What a man most enjoys about a woman's clothes are his fantasies of how she would look without them."

— BRENDAN FRANCIS

Full-length white cotton pique gown, with a scalloped hem, trimmed with red, a deep scoop neckline, puff sleeves and scalloped ruffles. Labeled *Lucie Ann, Beverly Hills, Nan Duskin*. *Courtesy of the Family of Bernice Harris*.

Full-length leopard print nylon set, with a sleeveless nightgown with deep V-neckline, and black lace insertion and trim on the bodice; short-sleeved dressing gown, with a three-button closure on the bodice and black lace trim. Labeled *Vanity Fair*. *Author's collection*.

Pink nylon shortie or mini-length sheer nightgown with a deep hem of beige lace and spaghetti straps; two-layered nightgown with a beige lace yoke and sleeves, pink satin trim and tie, and beige lace at the hem. Labeled *Claire Sandra, By Lucie Ann, Beverly Hills*. *Courtesy of the Family of Bernice Harris*.

"I think that's a very kinky issue with the panties and bras. That's the thing that they will display: shoes, panties, bras."

—IMELDA MARCOS

Kristen Kucharski models a full-length leopard print nylon nightgown, trimmed with black lace; the robe is draped behind her. *Courtesy of …20th C Apparel.*

Left, leopard print nylon half slip, with black lace at the hem. Labeled *Vanity Fair*; Right, Nylon/acetate step-in leopard print dressing gown, with long sleeves and a stand-up collar. Labeled *Butterfield 8, BU-8 INC.* *Author's collection*.

Butterfield 8, with Elizabeth Taylor, Laurence Harvy, and Edie Fischer, based on the novel by John O'Harra, was released in 1960. This line of lingerie was based on the film.

Left, pale blue layered ballerina-length nylon peignoir, with a wide beige lace collar, and a deep hem of beige lace. Labeled *Intime of California, 100% Nylon*, with original retail hangtag, *Fine's, Savannah – GA*; Right, beige layered nylon ballerina-length nightgown, with a beige lace bodice with an elevated waistline and satin ribbon detailing. Labeled *Vanity Fair*. *Author's collection*.

Full-length red silk dressing gown, with black silk appliqué up the front, on the sleeves in a saw-tooth design, with a reversible black and red silk tie at the waistline. Labeled *Made Expressly For Saks Fifth Avenue*. *Author's collection*.

Erin Clune models the red silk dressing gown, with black silk satin appliqué.

"I still can't believe that I walk down the runway once a year in high heels and underwear for Victoria's Secret, and that this is worthy of being broadcast on the Sony Jumbo Tron in Times Square."

—REBECCA ROMIJN STAMOS

White cotton eyelet lace garter belt, with nylon garters, and expandable spandex closure with metal hooks and eyes. Labeled *Crown-ette, Made In U.S.A.* Author's collection.

Young women of the 1950s and early 1960s wore cotton eyelet lace garter belts to hold up their stockings. Many of the garter belts of the period were just plain white cotton, and definitely not for show!

"The only gossip I'm interested in is things from the Weekly World News—'woman's bra bursts, 11 injured.' That kind of thing."

— JOHNNY DEPP

Very sheer ankle-length bright red nylon nightgown, with white straps with open work and rhinestones, and a sash at the midriff with silver leaf appliqué and rhinestones. Labeled *Lucie Ann Lingerie, Beverly Hills*. *Courtesy of the Family of Bernice Harris.*

LEFT:
Full-length pink nylon nightgown, with an elevated waistline, open back, and ruffles at the sleeves, neckline, and hem. Labeled *100% Nylon Tricot Satin. Author's collection.* Although the elevated or empire waistline has been fashionable in lingerie over several decades, going back to the Directoire and Empire periods of costume history, this style was particularly popular during the 1960s. The street wear equivalent was the baby doll dress.

Full-length white layered nylon peignoir, with delicate lace collar and cuffs. Labeled *Vassarette. Author's collection.*

BELOW:
Left, sheer blue nylon slip, trimmed on the bodice and at the hem with blue lace. Labeled *Warner's*;

Right, robin's egg blue nylon slip, with beige lace on the bodice and at the hem. Labeled *Van Raalte. Author's collection.*

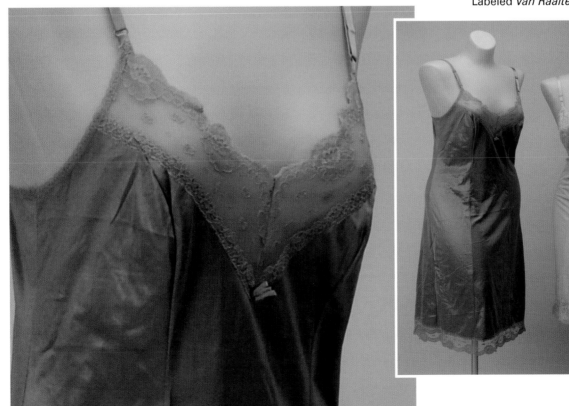

"I've always found that no matter what the design, most lingerie looks best on the floor by the bed."

—BLUESTRANGER
(CURRENT.COM)

Tess Stewart models black and white silk polka dot shortie nightgown by *Halston.* 1980s.

Aqua nylon crepe nightgown and matching robe, with elaborate ruffles, cape sleeves, a wide sash, and a rosette at the neckline of the nightgown. Labeled *La La's, Saks Fifth Avenue*. Courtesy of the Family of Bernice Harris.

Full-length white nylon tricot nightgown with navy blue velvet straps and sash, and an empire waistline. Labeled *Vanity Fair*. Courtesy of ...20th C Apparel.

Chapter 6
1970s

Full-length bright yellow nylon nightgown, with a long-sleeved, stretch lace bodice, with a small nylon bow at the deep V-neckline. Labeled *John Kloss for CIRA. Author's collection.*

John Kloss (1937 – 1987), winner of the Coty American Fashion Critics Award in 1971 and 1974, designed lingerie in vivid colors like lemon yellows, greens, amethyst, and ruby, and is known for his simple, clean designs, sometimes detailed with topstitching or tiny rows of buttons. His lingerie and loungewear was marketed by Lily of France and CIRA.

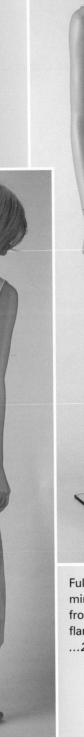

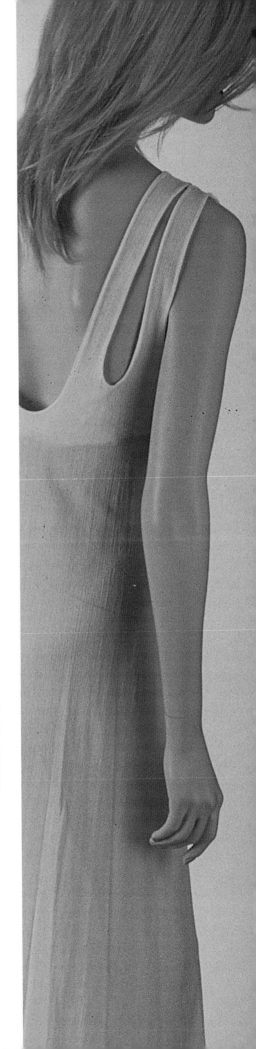

Full-length white crinkle crepe minimalist gown, with open work on front and back straps, and a slightly flared hem. Labeled *CIRA. Courtesy of ...20th C Apparel.*

Sheer nylon nightgown in a rose print in salmon pink on a black ground; one nightgown in a fitted style with a black lace and black satin bodice and spaghetti straps; a second nightgown, also in a rose print in salmon pink on a black ground, with a flowing style and black lace sleeves; matching peignoir with short, ruffled sleeves, a black nylon lining, and dyed black marabou feather trim. Labeled *Nan Duskin*. *Courtesy of the Family of Bernice Harris.*

Tyleah Miller models flared-leg, midriff-baring lounging pajamas from the 1970s, in a bold floral pattern, with a long-sleeved tie-front jacket. She is layering with a modern tee.

Full-length lilac velour robe, with gathers and ruffles at the neckline, and bows at the collar and cuffs of the three-quarter length dolman sleeves, in a pull-over style that flares at the hem. Labeled *Halston IV*, with original hangtag from *Nan Duskin*. *Courtesy of the Family of Bernice Harris.*

Calf-length purple silk charmeuse dressing gown, with all-in-one sleeves, in the minimalist style of its designer. Labeled *Zoran*. *Courtesy of …20th C Apparel.*

Two full-length nylon nightgowns showing design influence from earlier decades of costume history; Left, cinnamon color nylon, with an elevated waistline, laces, ruching, and wide shoulder straps. Labeled *Jody of California*. Right, pale pink nylon, with bishop sleeves, and a deep V-neckline with a panel of pink lace on the bodice. Labeled *Olga. Author's collection*.

Kristen Kucharski models nylon print nightgown, showing back.

Full-length sheer nylon print nightgown, in a tan, white and pink Oriental design, with an elevated waistline, a deep V-neckline, open back, and flared skirt. Labeled *Blanche*. *Author's collection*.

Full-length floral printed nylon dressing gown, in purple, blue, green, and white, with a matching sleeveless shortie nightgown. Labeled *Vera For Formfit Rogers*. *Courtesy of The Cats Pajamas Vintage.*

Yellow, pink, and orange bra and girdle set, in a stylized leaf and flower design; all nylon elastic with spandex. Labeled *Emilio Pucci For FR, Saks Fifth Avenue. Courtesy of The Cats Pajamas Vintage*.

Coral, blue, tan, brown, and pink bra and girdle set, in a stylized floral design; all nylon elastic with spandex. Labeled *Emilio Pucci For Formfit Rogers, Made In U.S.A.* Author's collection, purchased from *The Cats Pajamas Vintage*.

Pucci designed fascinating lingerie for Formfit Rogers during the 1960s and 1970s, including panties, bra and girdle sets, half slips, slips, nightgowns, and dressing gowns. Although the colorful geometric and stylized floral prints are the most collectible, many pieces are of solid colors, with contrasting or matching lace.

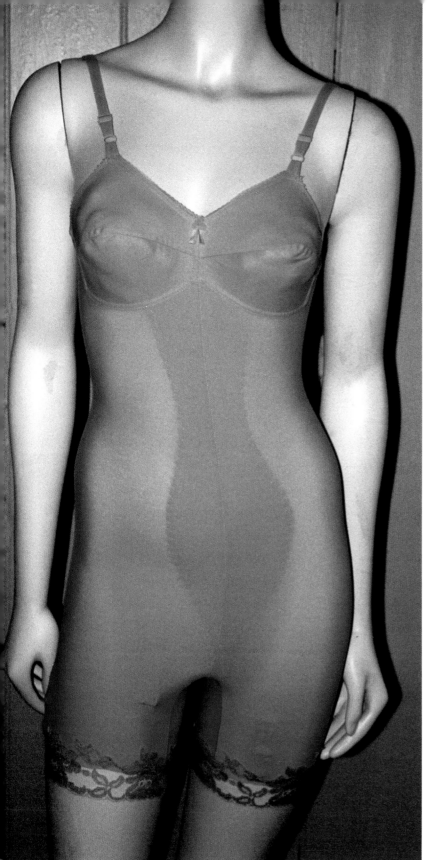

Blue nylon and spandex combination brassiere and panty girdle, with garters, crotch opening, and beige lace trim. Labeled *Van Raalte*. *Author's collection*.

Tan, brown, purple, and yellow panty girdle, in a stylized floral design; all nylon elastic with spandex. Labeled *Emilio Pucci For Formfit Rogers, Made In U.S.A. Courtesy of The Cats Pajamas Vintage*.

"You have to have the kind of body that doesn't need a girdle in order to pose in one."

—Carolyn Kenmore

Blue, fuchsia, and purple panty girdle, in a stylized floral design, nylon and spandex. Labeled *Saks Fifth Avenue, EPFR (Emilio Pucci Formfit Rogers)*, signature print. *Courtesy of The Cats Pajamas Vintage, each panty girdle pictured has soft, white elastic loops for garters.*

Colorful printed nylon half slip, with figures, faces, and architectural details, possibly of stained glass windows, in gold, green, orange, blue, and white. Labeled *Radiant, California, Radiant Fashions, Inc. Courtesy of The Cats Pajamas.*

Colorful printed nylon half slip, with geometric shapes in green, brown, hot pink, purple, and gold. Labeled *All Nylon. Courtesy of The Cats Pajamas Vintage.*

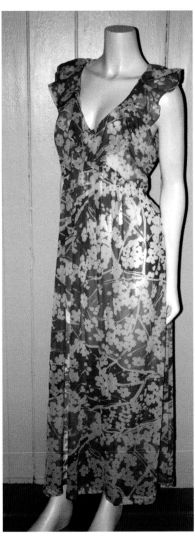

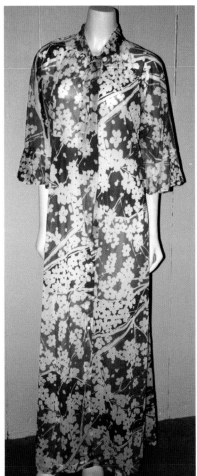

Full-length blue and white sheer nylon signature print *Vera* nightgown with ruffles at the neckline, and a matching full-length robe with elbow-length sleeves. *Courtesy of Nella Daniels.*

135

Chapter 7

1980s

Stretch lace was an important design element in lingerie of the 1990s. Used in teddies, gowns, slips and panties, skin-baring and provocative, stretch lace gave fashion designers the option of using lace at the sides of a garment, down the front, and symmetrically.

Full-length black and white silk geometric "H" print nightgown; sleeveless with a scoop neckline, narrow straps, and a slightly flared skirt with a 24-inch slit at one side. Labeled *Halston Intimates,* 100% silk. *Author's collection*.

Left, nylon half slip, with a panel of white lace up the front, and *DVF* monogram at the hem. Labeled *Diane Von Furstenberg*;

Right, aqua blue nylon ankle-length nightgown, with open, wrap style front and pale pink edging and monogram *DVF*.

Labeled *Diane Von Furstenberg For RE-7, Lord & Taylor. Author's collection*.

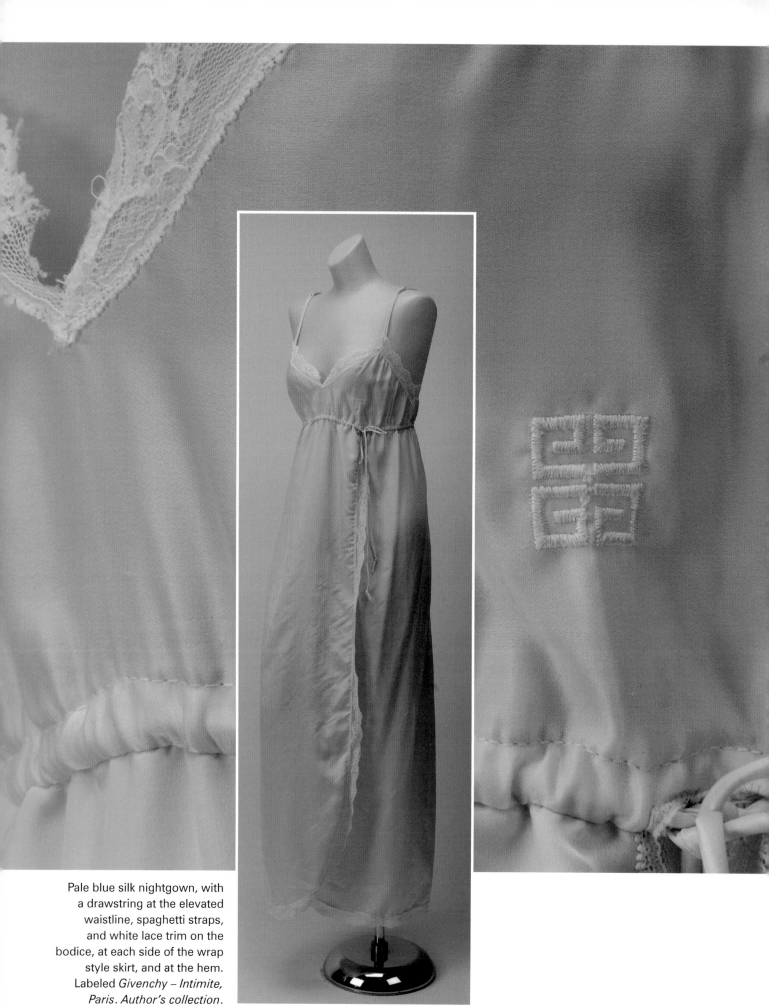

Pale blue silk nightgown, with a drawstring at the elevated waistline, spaghetti straps, and white lace trim on the bodice, at each side of the wrap style skirt, and at the hem. Labeled *Givenchy – Intimite, Paris. Author's collection*.

Red nylon and nylon lace combination or teddy. Designed by *Bob Mackie* for *Glydon's, Hollywood, Made In U.S.A. Author's collection*.

White nylon
and nylon lace
combination or
teddy with garters.
Designed with
narrow red ribbon
insertion, placed
vertically on each
side of a sheer
white lace front
panel. Labeled *Nan
Flower, 100% Nylon*.
Author's collection.

Shrimp pink ankle-length nylon
nightgown, with lace insertion
in a shell motif on the low cut
bodice, monogrammed *DVF*.
Labeled *Diane Von Furstenberg*.
Author's collection.

Full-length bright red silk wrap style dressing gown, with two "Harley Davidson Motor Cycles" insignias satin embroidered in blue and gold on the front, and a large, tan satin embroidered eagle on the back of the dressing gown atop the "Harley Davidson Motor Cycles" insignia. *Labeled 100% silk, Made In China. Courtesy of …20th C Apparel. A fascinating, specific interest dressing gown!*

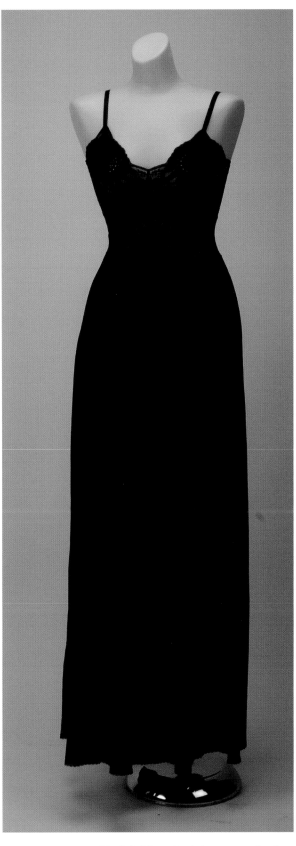

Black full-length nightgown, of nylon, polyester, silk stretch lace, and spandex. Designed by *Fernando Sanchez* for *Vanity Fair, Made In U.S.A. Author's collection.*

The American lingerie designer, Fernando Sanchez, signed with Vanity Fair in 1984 to design a moderately priced line of sleep and loungewear.

Full-length sea foam green satin nightgown and matching dressing gown, with ostrich plumes at the wrists of the long sleeves. Labeled *Lucie Ann of Beverly Hills for Nan Duskin*. Author's collection.

Kristen Kucharski models *Lucie Ann* nightgown and dressing gown.

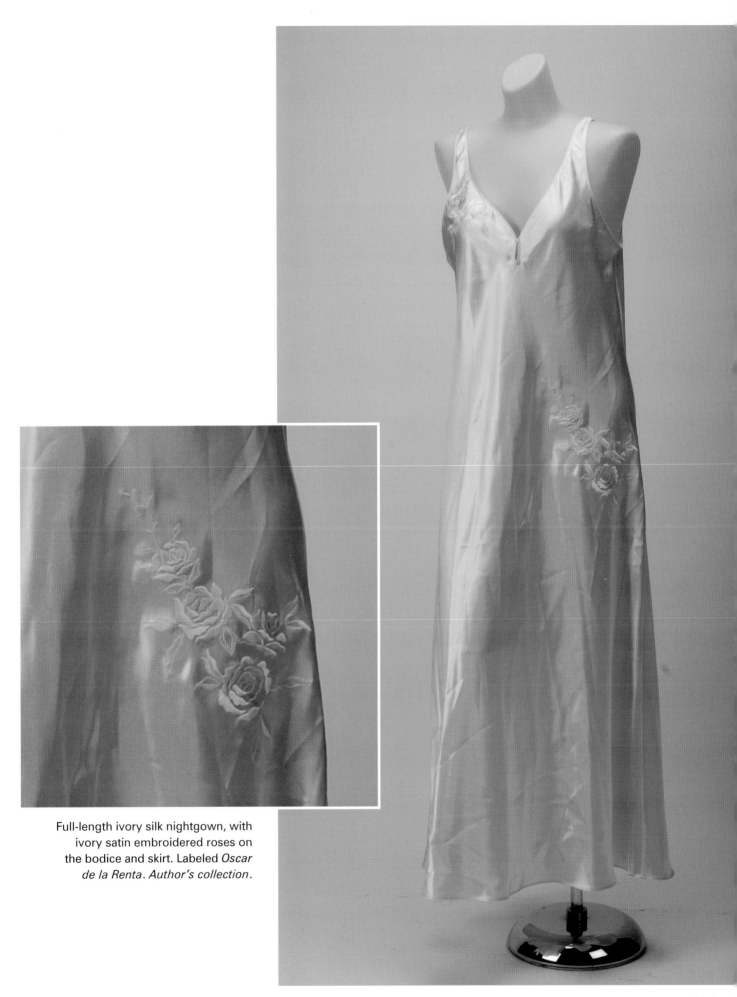

Full-length ivory silk nightgown, with ivory satin embroidered roses on the bodice and skirt. Labeled *Oscar de la Renta*. *Author's collection*.

Sheer blue nylon nightgown, with
matching string bikini panties, trimmed
with blue satin ribbon and beige lace.
Labeled *Frederick's Of Hollywood, 100%
Nylon. Author's collection.*

*Frederick Mellinger founded Frederick's
of Hollywood in 1946, with the belief that
incredible lingerie could make a woman
feel beautiful—from the inside out.*

"It's not what you wear –
it's how you take it off."

—Author Unknown

"You don't buy
black lingerie
unless
you want
someone to see it."

—BIANCA STRATFORD

Left, full-length black nylon nightgown, with revealing black lace bodice, low cut back, and flared skirt. Labeled *100% Nylon*; unworn with *Wear It Proudly, Made In U.S.A, By Your Neighbors*, and with original *John Wanamaker* retail price tag for $15;

Right, full-length black sheet nylon nightgown, with revealing black lace panels down the front, low cut front and back with black nylon spaghetti straps. Labeled *Circle III, New York*. *Author's collection.*

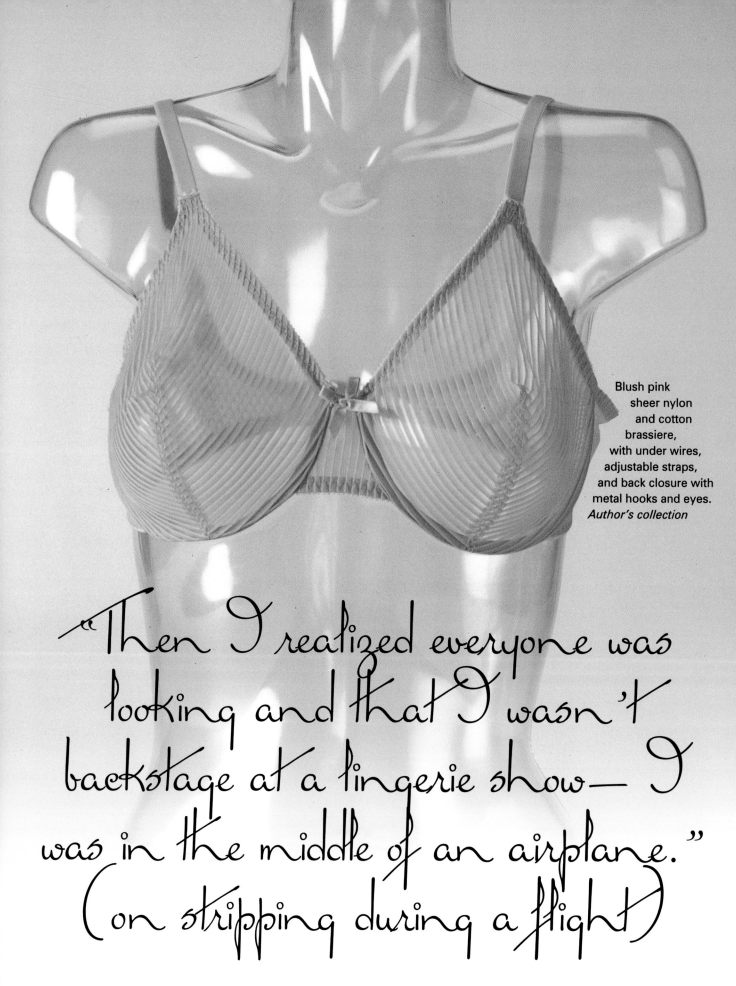

Blush pink
sheer nylon
and cotton
brassiere,
with under wires,
adjustable straps,
and back closure with
metal hooks and eyes.
Author's collection

"Then I realized everyone was looking and that I wasn't backstage at a lingerie show— I was in the middle of an airplane." (on stripping during a flight)

—TYRA BANKS.

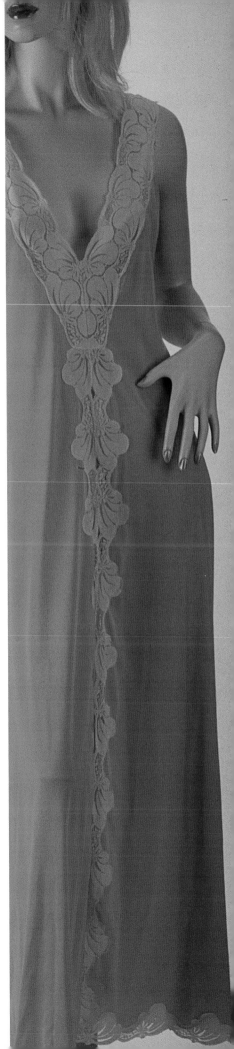

Coral pink nylon nightgown, with beige lace insertion, straps, and trim. Labeled *100% Nylon. Author's collection*.

Kristen Kucharski models coral pink nylon nightgown with beige lace.

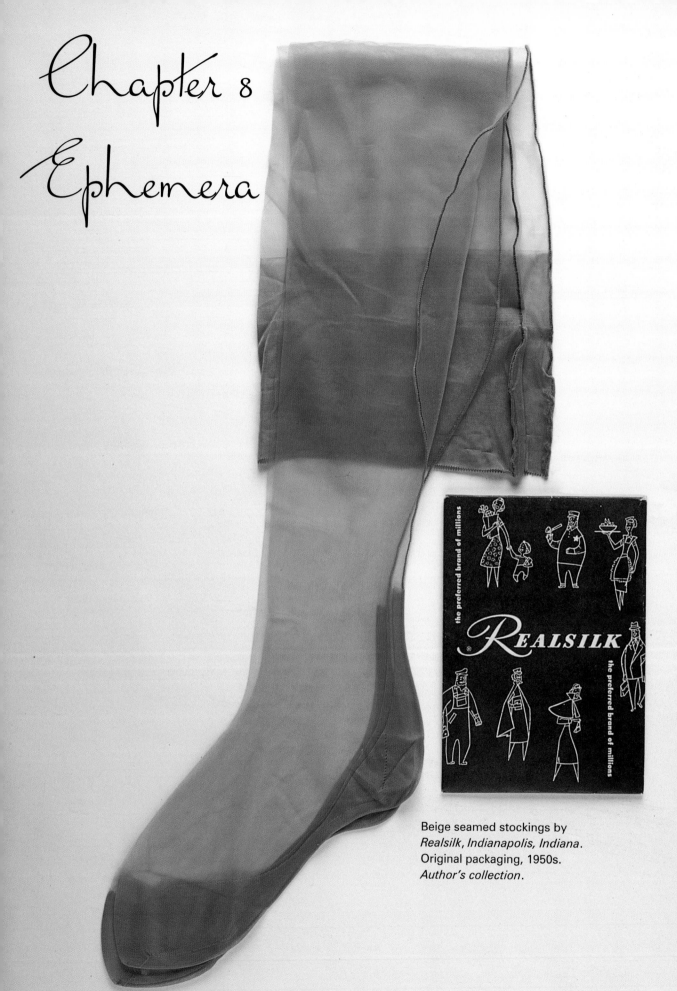

Chapter 8
Ephemera

Beige seamed stockings by
Realsilk, Indianapolis, Indiana.
Original packaging, 1950s.
Author's collection.

Detail of a *Slackette* label, for a satin combination designed to be worn with slacks, 1930s. *Courtesy of …20ᵗʰ C Apparel.*

Kristen Kucharski models a dark brown stretch jersey footed cat suit, with a diagonal yellow zipper that goes from front to back. *Courtesy of …20 C Apparel.*

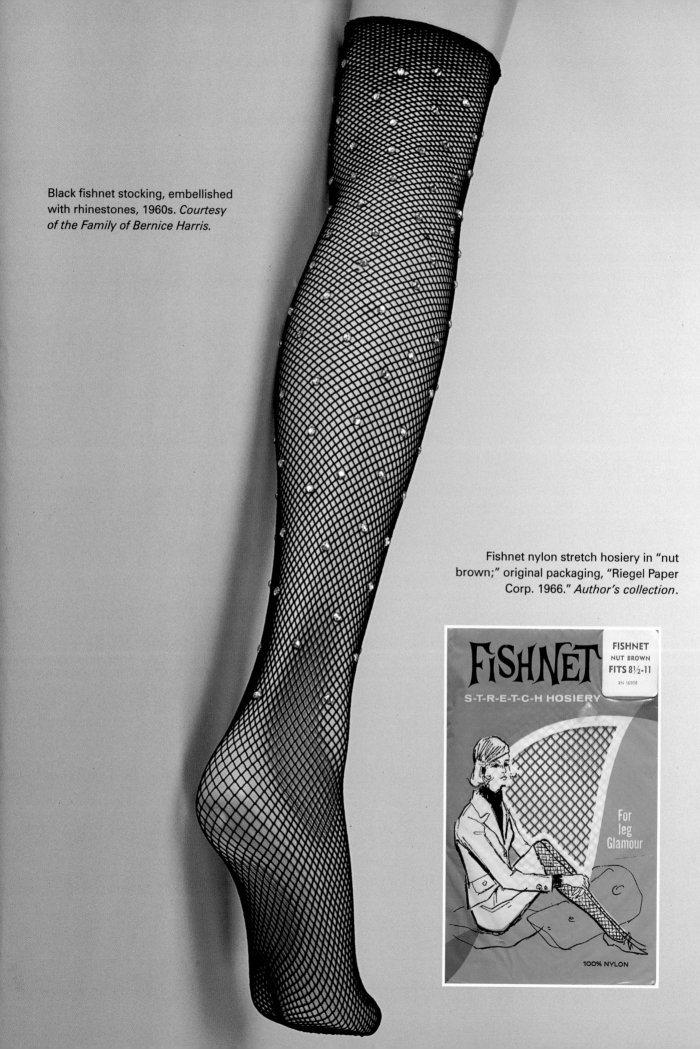

Black fishnet stocking, embellished with rhinestones, 1960s. *Courtesy of the Family of Bernice Harris.*

Fishnet nylon stretch hosiery in "nut brown;" original packaging, "Riegel Paper Corp. 1966." *Author's collection*.

FISHNET
S-T-R-E-T-C-H HOSIERY

FISHNET
NUT BROWN
FITS 8½-11
RN 16908

For leg Glamour

100% NYLON

Bra or slip adjustable shoulder straps, by *Gemco*. Original packaging, *Gem-Dandy, Inc., Madison, N. C.*, 1950s. *Author's collection.*

Vogue pattern for drawers, *Conde Nast Publications, Inc., New York*, 1940s. *Author's collection.*

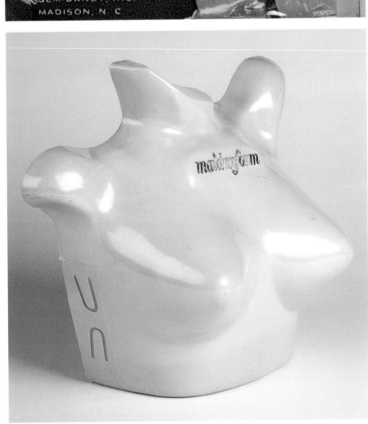

Sea foam green plastic display form, with raised navy blue letters, *maidenform*, 1950s. *Author's collection.*

155

what a smooth line..

. . . in a

*SHAR-LOO

"The Slip that Can't Slip!"

A smooth line that's not a lot of talk
but a matter of exclusive patented features:

1. Laton inserts mould bust, smooth waist.
2. Straight-cut front prevents twisting.
3. Bias-cut back prevents bulges.
4. Seamless sides prevent wrinkles.

Trillium-tailored of easy-to-launder rayon fabric.

$2.98 and $3.98 at all fine stores, or write TRILLIUM, Dept. V, 136 Madison Ave., New York 16, N. Y.
*reg. U. S. Pat. Off.

"Unmentionables—
those articles of ladies apparel
that are never discussed
in public, except in full-page,
illustrated ads."

— CHANGING TIMES

Lacy Slip perfectly sized just like your dr

Lacy Slip in Your Dress Size

Newest Textron Slip deeply edged and strapped with lovely lace.

Of snowy rayon satin, gleaming like white flowers against a shadow. Fits like your shadow, too, because Textron sized it exactly like your dresses. Not just at the bust alone, but at the waist and hipline, too. Just ask for your dress size . . . 12 to 20 average, 12 to 16 short . . new Textron idea to take the confusion out of slip buying. Choose Textron's lacy Dress Sized Slips in Snow White or Pink Angel. See many other Textron Dress Sized Slips . . . Textron-tailored from fiber to finished fashion . . . from $3.50 to $6 at leading stores throughout the country.

TEXTRON INC., Textron Building, 401 Fifth Avenue, New York 16, N. Y.

Bridal set, white rayon satin only • Cap-sleeved gown also in pink and white

C.J.Sternberg

Sweet as a proposal...smooth as wedding bells

Textron brings you blissful, beautiful lingerie.   A bridal white gown and bedjacket.   A dreamy "something blue"

to make an angel out of you!   All of finest, softest rayon . . . the bridal set in satin lush with lovely lace,

the cap-sleeved gown in crepe delicately detailed with piping.   Sizes 12 to 20.   Jackets: small, medium, large.

these romantic lingerie fashions, tailored with Textron's exquisite care, at leading stores throughout the country.

TEXTRON INC., Textron Building, 401 Fifth Avenue, New York 16, N. Y.

From filament to finished fashion

From the purr of spindles, the rhythm of thousands of looms comes the beautiful quality-controlled
fabric of your Textron slip today.   Textron puts this famous fabric through a rainbow of beautiful colorings.
Clicking cutters follow Textron's ingenious designs.   Buzzing stitchers tailor it with the same precision Textron
used in turning out parachutes—until it becomes the finished Textron masterpiece.   For quality blended
with the strength and beauty for which Textron is famous, ask to see Textron's breath-taking lingerie fashions.

HOME   FASHIONS

Silky-soft as a Dandelion Puff

Fairy-White enchantment for you. As soft and fresh as Spring's first breath—Textron's newest slip of finest, puff-soft rayon. Willow slim, to follow the lovely lines of your lovely figure. Cut, stitched and tailored with Textron's* famous parachute precision. In pretty Petal Pink and Midnight Black as well as pure Snow White. Sizes from 32 to 42. $2.95 at leading stores throughout the country.

TEXTRON INC., Empire State Building, Fifth Avenue, New York 1, N. Y.

TEXTRON
*REG. U. S. PAT. OFF.

HOSTESS COATS • MENSWEAR • LINGERIE

ah-h-h-h-h-

Creamy Pure Silk Satin

designed to be cherished (a Fischer
slip always is!). The bodice is
gentle flowered lace, and the slip
hues are cool, delicate. Champagne,
dove, larkspur blue, twilight gray
brown, pink, white, navy,
black or nude. At the
nicest stores near you.

Heavenly silk lingerie by Fischer

In quest of beauty!

Individual as your own peerless
taste, the quiet grandeur of a nightgown
by Fischer. Dreamed up for you in
silk par excellence...cap-sleeved
and bordered in a fine, rich lace.

Heavenly* silk lingerie   by Fischer

A garment to be cherished—
Gown or Slip by

Laros

Glossary

accordion pleats Folds in fabric that are named for their resemblance to the folds of the musical instrument called the accordion; smaller at the top and larger at the bottom.

adjustable Fit and appearance of garment can be changed or modified.

apparel Clothing of any type worn by men, women, and children.

Art Deco Based on a non-representational style in the arts of the 1920s and 1930s; relies on geometric and stylized forms.

Art Nouveau Designs emphasized curves, waves, stylized natural forms, and a strong sense of motion; based on the design period from 1890 to 1910, that related to artists and artisans trying to develop a style that did not rely on the past.

asymmetric Each side of the garment offers a different silhouette, as opposed to a balanced look.

at-home wear Clothing designed to be worn at home, particularly for entertaining.

baby-doll Garment cut like a smock, with a high neckline and gathers and pleats hanging from a tiny yoke.

backless Garment with an extremely low back, sometimes dipping to below the waist.

bandeau brassiere Made of two overlapping, triangular pieces of material held together across the back by a length of elastic, providing a snug fit and at the same time giving plenty of ease; offering slight support.

bandeau corset A variation of the bandeau brassiere, it is cut long enough to confine the hips slightly and also provide a foundation to which the hose supporters may be attached.

bare look Styles in which large areas of the body that are usually covered are revealed.

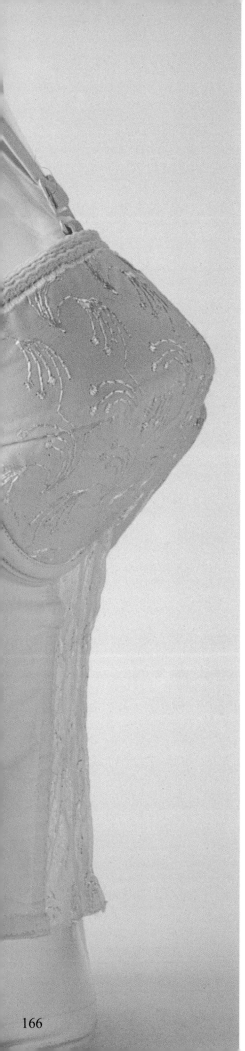

bare midriff Exposing the body from just under the bust to the waistline or hips.

bathrobe A garment that is practical, washable, and extremely serviceable; wraparound robe or dressing gown with long sleeves, a shawl collar, held closed with a sash.

bias The direction in fabrics diagonal to the lengthwise or crosswise directions.

bias-cut Designers use this technique for cutting clothing to use the greater stretch in the bias or diagonal direction of the fabric, causing it to accentuate body lines and curves and drape softly.

bloomer chemise Combines chemise and bloomers, with an upper section which is smooth and straight, and a lower section cut in a bloomer effect and gathered into bands just above the knees.

bloomers Full pants gathered at the hem.

body clothes Clothing that is tightly fitted, such as leotards, body stockings, and bodysuits.

body stocking One-piece, knitted body garment with legs and feet, with or without sleeves.

bodysuit One-piece, fitted garment, without legs, with long or short sleeves, or sleeveless, and snaps at the crotch.

brassiere Close fitting undergarment shaped to support and mold the breasts; usually with two cups, held in place with straps over the shoulders and elastic in the back.

caftan Full-length robe with a slit neckline and long or three-quarter-length sleeves; often embroidered at the neckline.

camisole-top chemise Top finished with a close fitting band, with wash ribbon shoulder straps, and tucks placed in groups for necessary fullness.

cascade Ruffles bias-cut from fabric, in a circular manner, falling in folds.

cat suit Tight-fitting, one-piece, long-sleeved suit, with attached "feet."

charmeuse A lightweight silk, cotton, or manufactured fiber dress fabric that is soft and drapes well. It is smooth, has a semi-lustrous satin face, and dull back.

chemise Loose combination undergarment for women, hanging straight from the shoulders and covering the torso.

cheongsam Chinese woman's dress which originated in Shanghai, China during the 1930s, and blends traditional Chinese and Western styles; basic design for housecoats, as well as dresses.

chiffon Plain weave, thin, transparent fabric that drapes well; originally made in silk, but now in manufactured fibers.

China silk Lustrous silk fabric in a plain weave; originally hand made in China, as early as 1200 B. C.

circular ruffle Cut from a circle of fabric rather than straight across the grain.

classic Style that continues to be fashionable for a long period of time; sometimes changed slightly, but retaining the basic lines of the original style.

combination Undergarment that combines vest and drawers; some garments of this type may have a crosswise joining at the waistline, or somewhat below it, while others have an opening down the center front and crosswise joining across the back only.

cording or cord Trimming made by inserting a soft, ropelike cord into a piece of bias-cut fabric; used for frogs and loops.

cotton Soft white vegetable fiber that comes from the fluffy boll of the cotton plant; grown in Egypt, India, China, and southern United States. Cotton fibers are absorbent, comfortable, and washable; often used for underwear and lingerie.

covered button Disk or ball-shaped button, covered with fabric which either matches or contrasts with garment.

crepe Fabrics with a grained or crinkled surface; may be made of silk, rayon, acetate, cotton, wool, and various manufactured fibers or blends.

crepe de chine Lightweight silk fabric with a crepe texture, made by using highly twisted yarns; may be printed or piece-dyed.

dart V-shaped tuck, used to make a garment conform to the contours of the body.

dishabille or dishabille Undress or negligent attire.

dotted swiss Crisp, sheer cotton fabric, ornamented with small dots distributed at regular intervals. There are two types of dotted swiss, that in which the dot is woven and that in which the dot is applied to the surface with an adhesive, such as flocking.

drape The extent to which fabric falls into graceful folds when hung or arranged in different positions; the technique of creating fashion designs by cutting and pinning fabric over a dress form.

drawers Trouser-like undergarments, undershorts, or underpants worn by both men and women.

ease Allowing extra measure when drafting a pattern, so that it will fit comfortably at bust, waist, and hips.

erogenous zone theory Well-known British authority on historic costume, James Laver, believed that emphasis on dress tends to shift from one erogenous zone of the body to another. For example, when plunging necklines are worn, the breasts are emphasized. In Laver's theory, there is a shift of interest from one zone to another about every seven years, and this is responsible for fashion change.

eyelet Circular metal ring which is clamped on fabric, through which cord or similar lacer is pulled.

faille Fabric with a flat-ribbed effect running crosswise that is less pronounced than grosgrain; made of silk, wool, cotton, manufactured fibers or combinations.

fastener Synonym for closure.

flounce Gathered or plaited strip sewn to garment; generally worn at the bottom of a garment, especially on skirt, sleeve, or cape.

frog Braid or cord fastener, through which a soft ball made of cord or a button is pulled; often used to fasten Chinese robes.

garter belt Elasticized band, which fits either around the hips or waist, and has four to six elastic garters attached to hold up hose.

godet Triangular piece of fabric, sometimes rounded at the top, flaring at the bottom; set into sleeve or skirt to give added fullness.

godet chemise Cut in two straight lengths of material, one full width and one from one-third to one-half width, depending on the size of the figure, and from the remainder of the width, cut two godets, or triangular inserts.

jumpsuit One-piece suit or combination of shirt and ankle-length pants, with zipper front and long or short sleeves; design based on flyers' and parachute jumpers' suits in World War II.

kimono Garment typical of Japanese costume, made as loose, wide-sleeved robe, fastened around the waist with a broad sash; negligee cut in the manner of a Japanese kimono.

laced closing Leather or cord laced through metal or embroidered eyelets.

leotard One-piece knitted garment with a high or low neckline, long or short sleeves, and brief style pants; based on similar garments worn by acrobat Jules Leotard in the 19th-century.

lingerie Women's underclothing, originally of linen, but now of dainty fabrics, such as silk, very often lace-trimmed or detailed with embroidery. The term was originally borrowed from the French language by Sarah Joseph Hale, the editor of *Godey's Lady's Book*.

loop and button Decorative fastening with a series of cord loops on one side and covered buttons on the other side.

mannish undergarment The garment features the same design and construction details as one of the popular styles worn by men and boys; top is cut lower than similar garment for men and boys.

marabou Soft tail and wing feathers of any of three storks of Africa or East Indies.

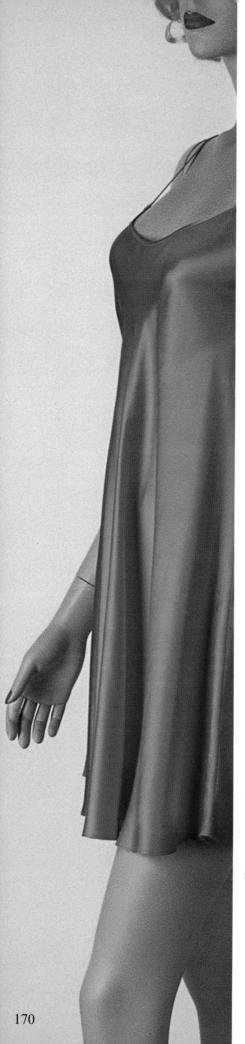

mother-of-pearl button Button made from the inside shell of the oyster, which is called nacre.

negligee Feminine, decorative dressing gown, generally with flowing lines, worn indoors by women.

nightgown or nightdress Sleeved or sleeveless chemise style garment, with soft details, worn while in bed.

pajamas Suit consisting of jacket or blouse and trousers; worn for sleeping, lounging, beach wear, depending on the style and fabric.

petticoat Undergarment for a woman or girl similar to a slip, but starting at the waist.

pettipants Long or dress-length underpants made of nylon or knits, often with ruffles or lace trimming, introduced in mid-1960s.

round-neck chemise Comfortably loose chemise, with shoulder straps as part of the garment.

side-dart chemise Simple straight-line chemise, close-fitting at the top and having the necessary fullness at the side in darts.

slip Under slip which is made the length of the dress with which it is to be worn; undergarment combining corset cover or brassiere and petticoat.

snap closure Metal fasteners used to fasten or close a garment.

step-ins Drawers of the step-in variety, similar to the lower part of a step-in chemise, except that they extend to the normal waistline; finish consists of a casing through which elastic is run.

stays Earlier term for corset, laced up the back with a scoop neckline in front and higher in back; made very rigid with iron or whalebone.

straight-line combination The lower part of this type of combination has no fullness, and there is a difference in cut, providing a concealed circular joining, which affords plenty of comfort, and at the same time achieves a slenderizing, straight-line effect.

tank top Design is similar to a man's undershirt, with a U-neckline, deep armholes, and narrow shoulder straps.

teddy Straight cut undergarment from the 1920s, combining a camisole with a short slip, or a long vest with underpants; has recently become a tight-fitting minimal garment with low-cut front and back.

tied closing A sash used on wrap style garments, such as robes, to hold the garment closed.

undress Ordinary dress for man or woman as contrasted with formal wear; term used in 18th and 19th centuries.

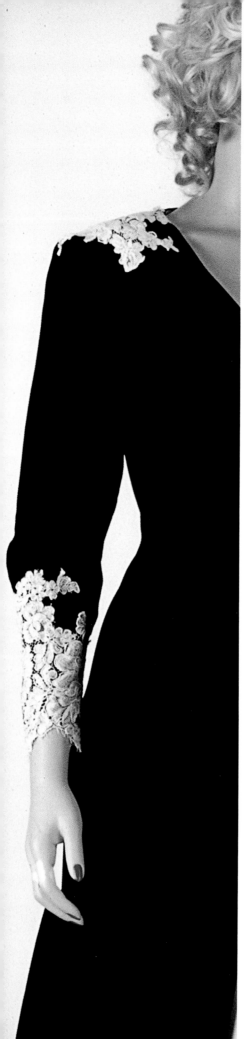

Bibliography

Calasibetta, Charlotte Mankey and Phyllis Tortora. *The Fairchild Dictionary of Fashion, Third Edition*. New York: Fairchild Publications, Inc., 2003.

Dior, Christian. *The Little Dictionary of Fashion*. New York: Abrams, 2007. (First published by Cassell & Co. Ltd., 1954)

Ewing, Elizabeth. *Dress & Undress*. London: B. T. Batsford Ltd., 1989.

Laver, James. *Costume and Fashion: A Concise History, Fourth Edition*. London: Thames & Hudson Ltd., 2007.

Picken, Mary Brooks. *A Dictionary Of Costume And Fashion: Historic And Modern*. Mineola, New York: Dover Publications, Inc., 1985.

Tortora, Phyllis G. and Keith Eubank. *Survey of Historic Costume: A History of Western Dress. 5th Edition.* New York: Fairchild Publications, 2009.

Underwear And Lingerie, Parts I & 2. The Woman's Institute of Domestic Arts And Sciences, Scranton, PA. International Textbook Company, Scranton, PA, 1925, 1926, 1930.

Vassiliev, Alexandre, *Beauty in Exile*, New York: Harry N. Abrams, Inc., Publishers, 2000.

Internet sources

www.current.com

www.quotationspage.com

www.thinkexist.com

Suggested Reading

Apsan, Rebecca, with Sarah Stark. *The Lingerie Handbook*. New York: Workman Publishing, 2006.

Barbier, Muriel and Shazia Boucher. *The Story of Lingerie*. New York: Parkstone Press USA, December 2004.

Berry, Cheree. *For The Bra: A Perky Peek at The History Of The Brassiere*. New York: Stewart, Tabori & Chang, 2006.

Glanville-Blackburn, Jo. *A Passion For Lingerie*. New York: Ryland Peters & Small, 2005.

Steele, Valerie. *The Corset: A Cultural History*. New Haven & London: Yale University Press, 2005.

Pedersen, Stephanie. *Bra: A Thousand Years Of Style, Support And Seduction*. United Kingdom: David & Charles, 2004.

Resources

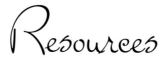

Alderfer Auction Company, Auctioneers/Appraisers, Hatfield, Pennsylvania, www.alderferauction.com. Holds live auctions of vintage and designer clothing and accessories.

Shelley Brice-Boyle, Sweet Cherry Vintage Lingerie Boutique, www.sweetcherryvintage.com. email: shelley@sweetcherryvintage.com. West Coast dealer specializing in vintage lingerie.

The Cats Pajamas, www.catspajamas.com, email ("Miss Kitty"): catspajamasvintage@gmail.com. Wonderful online collection, offering vintage clothing and accessories; source for the Emilio Pucci underwear.

The Costume Society of America, www.costumesocietyamerica.com, works to "stimulate scholarship and encourage study in the rich and diverse field of costume". The CSA publishes the educational journal, *Dress,* and provides important seminars and costume-related opportunities for its members, as well as a calendar of costume exhibitions at museums throughout the United States.

Pamela Daly, Faded Frocks Vintage Clothing and Textiles, www.etsy.com/shop/fadedfrocks, email: rustyrosepetals@aol.com.

Nella Daniels, email: nelladaniels@msn.com.

Svetlana Davydova, www.lanasworks.com, sdavydova@hotmail.com, Professional textile restorer. A member of the CSA, Ms. Davydova specializes in restoration, conservation, and on-site consulting.

enokiworld, www.enokiworld.com, high level vintage and designer clothing and accessories, often has Emilio Pucci for Forfit Rogers.

Doris Hoagland, Sammyjoco2, email: sammyjoco2@comcast. net

Carol and Dwayne Kowerdovich, email: viva1@verizon.net. Vintage clothing and accessories, including fine vintage lingerie.

Kristen Kucharski, Missy Model, email: missyfitmodel@gmail. com.

Maire McCleod, http://elegantvintage.com/. and elegantly designed website, offering fine lingerie; email: marymcleod@yahoo. com.

Silver Screen Loungerie, www.silverscreenloungerie.com, offers fine vintage lingerie with an aura of old Hollywood glamour; excellent descriptions by Sascha Joffe and Richard Reissig.

Barry S. Slosberg, Inc., Auctioneers/Appraisers, www.bssauction. com, info@bssauction.com. Holds live auctions of vintage clothing and accessories several times each year.

Vintage Fashion Guild, www.vintagefashionguild.org, an online international collaborative. A fascinating source of information about vintage clothing and accessories, VFG offers, under the category "explore vintage fashion," The Lingerie Resource, with "an ever growing compilation of lingerie terms, with photos of garments by Vintage Fashion Guild members. Although selective, membership is open to non-vendors.

Vintage Textile, www.vintagetextile.com, an online source of high style antique, designer, and vintage clothing and accessories, including early lingerie. Email Linda Ames, Linda@vintagetextile. com.

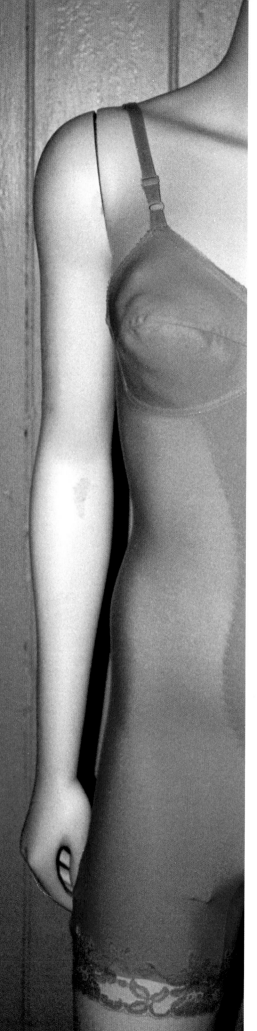

Index